ST. MARY'S COLLEGE OF MARYLAND
SL MARY'S CITY, MARYLAND

INNOCENT III
CHVRCH DEFENDER

050884

CHARLES EDWARD SMITH

INNOCENT III
CHVRCH DEFENDER

GREENWOOD PRESS, PUBLISHERS
WESTPORT, CONNECTICUT

Copyright 1951 by Louisiana State University Press

Reprinted with the permission
of Louisiana State University Press, Baton Rouge

First Greenwood Reprinting 1971

Library of Congress Catalogue Card Number 79-88939

SBN 8371-3145-6

Printed in the United States of America

INTRODUCTION

J UDGED by actual accomplishment, the Medieval Papacy reached its apogee in the pontificate of Innocent III. Young, vigorous, steeped in theology and the Roman Law, Lothario de Segni brought to the papal office administrative ability, political and diplomatic acumen, and an exalted conception of his responsibilities scarcely equaled in the history of the Petrine See.

Reform was a major objective during Innocent's entire pontificate. Again and again he asserted that since he ultimately would be held to account for the shortcomings of all Christians, upon him devolved a direct obligation to initiate correctional measures or to bolster the reform efforts of the subordinate prelacy. Only if the Church was above reproach could the strictures of the heretics be refuted and the allegiance of the laity retained; only by clerical dedication to the extirpation of abuses could secular princes be compelled to respect the Church's privileges and immunities. A great cause beckoned devoted sons of a reinvigorated and militant Church—the liberation of the Holy Land. For this the pope pledged his every energy; for this he labored to ensure peace and political stability throughout the Christian world.

The Fourth Lateran Council, which the pope fondly believed would inaugurate a triumphant Crusade, epitomized the reform efforts of his pontificate in its memorable canons. Yet it is only from study of the actual cases that necessitated papal intervention that we gain a realization of the magnitude of the reforming task. In the complicated details, in the welter of appeals, charges, and rebuttals, we see the pope unremittingly struggling, often in the face of the apathy of local prelates, against the forces of evil. Most of the pontiff's letters bear the unmistakable stamp of his personal authorship, as by Biblical citation and homily he insisted upon the observance of the law—always, however, with keen appreciation of equity.

Full-length biographies of Innocent III as well as detailed treatments of special phases of his pontificate are available in considerable number, as indicated by the bibliographical note at the end of this study. Therefore, papal intervention in cases that have received authoritative treatment will only be mentioned in this discussion. Likewise, the story of the Fourth Crusade prior to the capture of Constantinople will only be outlined, while Innocent's lesser-known activities after 1204 will be more thoroughly presented. If this procedure results in some distortion of perspective for the general reader, it perhaps will be justified by the avoidance of repetition of material with which students of the period are completely familiar. Emphasis upon evils and papal efforts to carry out reforms also presents a danger of distortion. It therefore should constantly be borne in mind that offending clergy constituted only a very small minority of the ecclesiastical personnel; the exceptional nature of the cases in which they were involved was attested by the direct intervention of the Holy See.

In our times there is abundant evidence that the struggle of the Church against oppression and spoliation is a perennial one. Again prelates are persecuted, churches ring with the jeers of the godless, and the forces of secularism are arrayed against Christians throughout much of the world. In such a period the courage and energy with which Innocent III defended the Church against similar evils in his day may serve as an encouragement and inspiration.

Contents

Contents

CHAPTER I

A VIOLENT AGE

INNOCENT, DEFENDER OF THE CLERGY

PROBABLY no pope in the history of the Medieval Church more successfully asserted his power over secular rulers than did Innocent III. With the decisive victory at Bouvines in 1214, Frederick II, young Hohenstaufen ward of the pope, vindicated his claim to the throne of the Holy Roman Empire and thus ensured the triumph of one of Innocent's most cherished policies. King John of England, forced to recognize the pope's appointee, Stephen Langton, as Archbishop of Canterbury, ultimately agreed to hold his kingdom in feudal tenure as a vassal of the Holy See. Philip Augustus of France was compelled, at least outwardly, to recognize Ingeburga as his wife and queen in the celebrated marital case. Alfonso IX, King of León, and Ottocar II, King of Bohemia, also were forced to yield to papal mandates in enforcement of the sanctity of the marriage vow.

But Innocent's struggles with powerful laymen were by no means confined to kings and princes. The Petrine See, he insisted, was the mother and protector of all churches and of all the clergy. The primacy of Rome entailed not only power and prestige but also commensurate responsibility, and unflagging vigilance therefore had to be exercised to protect the Church against all aggressions. Failure to intervene forcibly in support of local ecclesiastical officials, Innocent believed, would be tantamount to acquiescence in iniquity. No plea for aid remained unanswered, therefore, no matter how exalted the offender or how lowly the rank of the clerical victim of violence or spoliation.

An object of Innocent's constant solicitude was the protection of the persons of the clergy against violence. Assaults upon clerics were punished by excommunication, in accordance with the canons of the Lateran Councils of 1097 and 1139 and the bull *Si quis suadente diabolo* of Innocent II (1130–1143). Whenever necessary or expedient the excommunication was accompanied by the imposition of an interdict on the lands of the offender. The gravity of the penalty also normally was enhanced by the stipulation that absolution of those excommunicated for laying violent hands upon the clergy could be secured only by personal appearance before the Roman Curia. It was believed that the difficulties and expense of such a journey to Rome would be a powerful deterrent, although the rigor of the law frequently was relaxed by dispensations authorizing local absolution if equity seemed to warrant such clemency.[1]

From his predecessor, Celestine III, Innocent inherited the problem of securing the liberation of the Archbishop of

---

[1] J. P. Migne (ed.), *Patrologiae cursus completus, Series Latina,* 221 vols. (Paris, 1884–1891), CCXIV, cols. 269–70. This work is hereinafter cited as *P.L.* For a good general estimate of the pontificate see Felix Rocquain, *La cour de Rome et l'esprit de reforme avant Luther* (Paris, 1893), 346, 414; Alberto Serafini, *I precedenti storici del concilio Lateranense IV (1215), Innocenzo III e la riforma religiosa agli inizii del sec. XIII* (Rome, 1917), *passim.* I am appreciative of the courtesy of the University of Chicago Press for permission to use material from my article, "Clerical Violence in the Pontificate of Innocent III," *Journal of Religion,* XXIV (1944), 424–27. I also am indebted to the American Catholic Historical Association for permission to incorporate sections from my article, "Innocent III; Defender of the Clergy," *The Catholic Historical Review,* XXII (1947), 415–29.

Salerno, who had been taken as a prisoner into Germany during the outbreak of civil strife in Sicily precipitated by the death of the emperor, Henry VI (1197). In a letter addressed to the bishops of Spires, Augsburg, and Worms, Innocent declared that the Lord Himself indicated how grievous was the sin of those who raised their hands against the clergy when He declared that He was persecuted in the person of His ministers. The sentence of excommunication applied not only against persons actually guilty of violence against clerics but also against those who tacitly condoned the crime by refusal to shun those under the ban of the Church.

The bishops were directed to bring further pressure to bear by publicly repeating the sentence of excommunication. If Wicel de Berc, who had been most responsible for the archbishop's detention, did not immediately seek absolution, he was to be shorn of all his benefices, while territory in which the prelate was held a prisoner or to which he might subsequently be taken was to be placed under an interdict. Indeed, all princes of Germany were warned that unless they exerted their every resource to ensure the archbishop's release, the interdict would be made general throughout Germany.[2]

Philip of Swabia already had been excommunicated by Celestine III because of his seizure of papal lands in Tuscany. The duke had manifested his desire for absolution, but was told that it could not be granted by anyone save the pope. Nevertheless, if Philip was instrumental in bringing about the release of the imprisoned Archbishop of Salerno, Innocent declared that the requirement for seeking absolution at Rome would be waived.[3] This offer by the

<hr />

[2] Migne (ed.), *P.L.*, CCXIV, col. 19.   [3] *Ibid.*, col. 20.

pope proved effective, for the archbishop was released largely as a result of Philip's intercession.[4]

Another flagrant case of outrageous violence against a high clerical official was incident to the civil war between Philip of Swabia and Otto of Brunswick. "Sons of Belial," who were partisans of Philip, organized a conspiracy to murder Conrad, Bishop of Würzburg, a supporter of Otto. The conspirators, who hitherto, "like Judas," had concealed their enmity toward the prelate, broke into his church "like wolves into a sheepfold." After seizing the bishop, they cut off his right arm, "the very arm with which he had consecrated the bread and wine into the Body of the Lord." They then consummated the foul assault by decapitating the prelate and cutting off his tonsure, "despite the fact that it contained the holy oil of consecration." The mutilated body then was "exposed as food to birds and beasts of prey" to flaunt the crime before the populace of the diocese.[5]

In a letter to Eberhard, Archbishop of Salzburg, in regard to this horrible affair, Innocent declared that no sadness was comparable with that of the Church whose sons were killed by the workers of iniquity. If such outrages could be perpetrated with impunity against prominent clergy, what authority would the lawless recognize? No member of the clergy would be safe, for the murder of a prelate would embolden others to emulate the sacrilege of the criminals. The archbishop was ordered to announce every Sunday and feast day the excommunications of those involved in the crime, with bell and candle to impart additional solemnity. Interdicts were to be imposed on the lands

[4] "Gesta Innocentii Tercii," in Migne (ed.), *P.L.*, CCXIV, cols. xxxiii–xxxviii.

[5] *Ibid.*, col. 1167; Richard Schwemer, *Innocenz III und die deutsche Kirche während des Thronstreites von 1198–1208* (Strassburg, 1882), 53–54.

of all implicated in the murder, with only baptism and extreme unction permitted; and the inquisitorial method of investigation was invoked to attempt to discover the identity of the assailants.[6] The ensuing investigation apparently did not ferret out the criminals, with the result that the pope had to be content with the general sentence.

Another shocking case occurred in the parish of Caithness, Scotland, where a group of scoundrels subjected the bishop of the diocese to torture, even cutting out his tongue. The ringleader of the hoodlums fortunately was apprehended, and the pope, to whom the crime was reported, personally prescribed the severe penance to be performed by the culprit. Clad only in trousers and a sleeveless woolen coat and carrying a green bough, the offender was required to walk for fifty days about the diocese in which his crime had been perpetrated. During the fifty-day period his tongue was to be kept tied by twine except while he ate his meals, limited to bread and water. Upon conclusion of the penitential perambulations the culprit was to prostrate himself before the cathedral of the mutilated bishop to undergo a severe flogging with the bough he had carried. Then he was ordered to go to the Holy Land for two years to perform such hard labor for the benefit of the holy places as might be directed by local ecclesiastical authorities. His fast on bread and water was to continue during the entire period unless amelioration might prove necessary as a concession to physical frailty.[7]

In 1206, Duke Wladislav of Poland aroused Innocent's wrath by a series of violent acts against the clergy. In a letter of bitter recrimination the pontiff declared that the duke had not been invested with the sword of secular authority

---

[6] Migne (ed.), *P.L.*, CCXIV, cols. 1167–70.   [7] *Ibid.*, cols. 1062–63.

in order to plunge it into the body of his mother, the Church. He had not been placed over his subjects to lead them in attacks upon their pastors, and he need only recall the examples of Old Testament kings to realize how grievously he was offending God. Henry, Archbishop of Gniezno, had been kept a prisoner in his own cathedral by the duke's orders; indeed, the canons had been forced to stand guard over their prelate since his incarceration. Other clergy had been imprisoned, even tortured, while relics of churches had been seized and ecclesiastical property confiscated.[8] The duke was peremptorily ordered to release the archbishop and to make amends for all his offenses. The pope's mandates apparently were effective, for the duke's absolution was soon announced in a papal letter stating that he had made suitable atonement.[9]

In January, 1207, the pope wrote another strong letter to Wladislav. The aggressions of the duke against the clergy actually constituted serious molestation of the pope himself, Innocent declared. The pontiff, "bound to favor God more than man," accordingly confirmed the ecclesiastical sentence promulgated against the duke by the Archbishop of Gniezno because of each and all of the offenses committed against the liberty of the Church. The bishops of Prague, Olmütz, and Meissen were directed to join their efforts with those of the Polish prelates to bring about the duke's submission. The excommunication proclaimed against the offender was ordered repeated with bell and candle each Sunday and feast day.[10] Again the pope's mandates were effective, for the duke's absolution was announced in a letter

[8] *Ibid.*, CCXV, cols. 1060–62; 1062–63.　　　　[9] *Ibid.*, col. 1059.
[10] E. G. Gersdorf and C. F. von Posern-Klett (eds.), *Codex diplomaticus Saxoniae regiae,* 3 vols. in 4 (Leipzig, 1864), II, 73.

stating that suitable penance had been performed for all offenses.

The duke's contrition was short-lived, for in 1211 the pope ordered the Bishop of Halberstadt to take measures to restrain the Polish ruler's excesses. The Archbishop of Gniezno had complained that Wladislav, ignoring the prelate's remonstrances, had seized archiepiscopal treasures, burned manor houses, and despoiled the clergy of the province of sundry properties. When the archbishop attemped to go to Rome personally to appeal for Innocent's help, the duke allegedly prevented him by force from doing so. But the ecclesiastical censures imposed upon the duke for his earlier offenses apparently were not renewed, and the absence of further action by the pope indicates that at least nominal compliance with his orders was secured.[11]

Sporadic violence against the clergy in Hungary occasioned papal intervention from the beginning of Innocent's pontificate. In July, 1199, the pope wrote to King Henry, pointing out that Hungary was held in especially high esteem by the Holy See because of the merit of its kings, shown particularly by the fervent devotion of the late King Bela, Henry's father. In view of this tradition of reverence for the Apostolic See, Innocent had hoped for the same piety from Henry; yet the more the pope favored the king the more grievous had been the reports of his conduct.

While the Bishop of Csanád was saying Mass in his cathedral, the king and his retainers had rushed into the church and demanded the keys of the sacristy. When the bishop and his canons thereupon began to chant a psalm to enlist the Lord's aid, Henry became so enraged that he rushed up to the altar and hurled the prelate to the floor.

[11] Migne (ed.), *P.L.*, CCXVI, col. 413.

He then dragged the bishop along the floor and cast him out of the cathedral.

After this outrageous assault the king seized diocesan properties and announced the sequestration of property the bishop recently had given to a monastery, apparently the original cause of the royal wrath. The bishop ordered cessation of church services in the diocese, although no formal interdict apparently was proclaimed; the monarch retaliated by ordering suspension of payment of all tithes. When Henry subsequently learned of the bishop's plans to send envoys to the pope, the emissaries were threatened with being blinded if they dared attempt to leave the kingdom.

Innocent wrote directly to the king in response to the bishop's letter of complaint, which reached its destination despite efforts to prevent an appeal. Henry was ordered to restore the bishop to immediate possession of his properties and to make satisfaction for the outrages committed. Otherwise, the pope declared, he was bound by the nature of his office and priestly calling to love God more than man and therefore could not hesitate to invoke the "ultimate powers of the Church." [12] Sauli de Hedevar, Archbishop of Kalocsa, was ordered by separate letter to ensure obedience to the pope's mandates. [13]

In a subsequent letter to Henry the pope declared that the Church hitherto had been held in great reverence in the Hungarian kingdom, so that even a thief resorting to its asylum was protected. But now the traditional freedom which the Church had enjoyed was jeopardized by those who "neither knew nor cared how perilous it was to have no fear of the Lord." Not only guilty fugitives but even

[12] *Ibid.*, CCXIV, cols. 643–45.   [13] *Ibid.*, col. 645.

persons innocent of wrongdoing were violently seized in churches, and sacred objects deposited in the edifices for safekeeping were stolen. The pope therefore ordered the archbishops of Gran and Kalocsa to procure the prompt restoration of all the liberties of the Hungarian Church and clergy, if necessary, by imposing interdicts.[14] The king was ordered to render every possible assistance to the prelates.[15]

The pope's intercession greatly improved conditions; but in 1213 he was informed that criminals in Hungary, among other offenses, had flogged and otherwise maltreated clergy of the archdiocese of Gran. Excommunication of these malefactors with bell and candle was ordered for each feast day,[16] and all nobles were warned not to harbor the culprits if they fled into their domains.[17]

One of the most severe punishments meted out to those guilty of violence against the clergy was the requirement of coming to Rome in person for absolution. As the pope stated in a letter to Geoffrey, Archbishop of Tours, laics guilty of invading the houses or properties of clergy, of illegal detention of legacies, or of extortion would be subject to excommunication with bell and candle. Such offenders could be absolved locally; those guilty of laying violent hands upon clerics, however, would have to come to Rome to make their peace.[18]

Yet the rigor of this stipulation was frequently relaxed at the behest of local ecclesiastical authorities. When Peter, Archbishop of Compostella, requested papal permission to absolve penitents excommunicated for violence against the

---

[14] *Ibid.*, col. 368.   [15] *Ibid.*   [16] *Ibid.*, CCXVI, col. 950.
[17] August Theiner (ed.), *Vetera monumenta historica Hungariam sacram illustrantia*, 2 vols. (Rome, 1859), II, 95.
[18] J. H. Geslin de Bourgogne and Anatole de Barthelmy (eds.), *Anciens evêches de Bretagne*, 4 vols. (Paris and St. Brieuc, 1855–1864), III, 229–30.

persons of clerics, Innocent declared that he considered the prelate a good shepherd, "who carried his sheep back to the fold on his shoulders, and, by diligent solicitude, guarded them in their helplessness." In view of the confidence he reposed in the archbishop's discretion, the pope authorized him to extend such absolutions, provided the beneficiaries of special favor took a solemn oath to refrain from violence in the future. Flagrant cases, however, the archbishop was directed to reserve for papal action "lest the nerve of ecclesiastical discipline, which is excited by violence, be paralyzed by lack of use." [19]

Dispensation from the onerous requirement of coming to Rome was granted on several occasions to those who by reason of age or infirmity were unable to withstand the rigors of the journey, and concessions also were extended to women in deference to their frailty.[20] In the case of several offenders in Sicily the pope acknowledged that the hot climate was conducive to fits of temper and a consequent increase in the number of cases of violence against churchmen. Since he sought only the immunity of the clergy and the salvation of sinners, the pope declared that he would pay special heed to the biblical injunctions to pray for persecutors and would be especially lenient.[21]

Another factor justifying dispensation from the requirement of coming to Rome for absolution was cited in the case of several scholars of the University of Paris who had incurred penalties by striking clerics. The Abbot of St. Victor claimed that a journey to Rome would entail serious detriment to the scholarship of the students involved because

[19] Migne (ed.), *P.L.*, CCXV, col. 85.
[20] *Ibid.*, CCXIV, col. 269; CCXV, cols. 85–86.
[21] *Ibid.*, CCXIV, cols. 269–70.

of the instruction they would miss, aside from the expense, which might so deplete their financial resources as to interfere with the continuance of their studies. Innocent, in reply, authorized the abbot to grant the dispensations unless the offenses were unusually serious, but this clemency was not applicable to students sentenced for offenses committed outside Paris.[22]

Cases sometimes arose in which lay officials employed violence against criminous clerks in a sincere effort to enforce ecclesiastical discipline. Peter Munnoz, Archbishop of Compostella, informed the pope that two justiciars in his province, renowned for their zeal for law enforcement, had arrested clerics and treated them like lay offenders. In the mistaken belief that their office entailed not only the right but the duty to proceed against clerical transgressors, the justiciars had refused to heed the archbishop's remonstrances. The prelate further pointed out that any effort to force the officials to come to Rome for absolution from the excommunication they had incurred would likely provoke serious trouble. In response to the archbishop's request for advice Innocent declared that a good pastor tries to call, rather than to drive, errant sheep back into the fold; if excessive severity were employed against them, they might fall into a pit instead of coming to receive healing treatment. He therefore authorized the archbishop to absolve the justiciars, with the proviso that the money they would have spent for the cost of the journey to Rome be donated to the Christian cause in the Holy Land.[23]

In a somewhat similar case in the archdiocese of Lund the pope ruled that if laymen used violence against criminous clerks who could not otherwise be apprehended, no

[22] *Ibid.*, CCXVI, col. 510.   [23] *Ibid.*, CCXV, cols. 84–85.

guilt was incurred if they acted in response to a mandate from proper ecclesiastical authority. Nevertheless, laymen were not to employ violence beyond that absolutely necessary either for their own defense or to ensure the apprehension and safe custody of incorrigible clerks.[24]

Embarrassment sometimes arose when servants of prominent ecclesiastics committed acts of violence against churchmen. The Archbishop of Bourges represented to the pope that several of his servants, excommunicated for this offense, had been ordered to Rome for absolution. The expenses of such a journey would fall upon the Church, however, since the penitents had no funds of their own. Then, too, the archbishop would be deprived of their services until the journey was completed, and this was equivalent to additional economic loss to the Church. As further extenuation for clemency, the archbishop regretfully admitted that his clergy had not set an edifying example, since they had often struck each other within sight of the servants; indeed, "it was impossible to tell whom the devil might tempt to commit such a sin." In his desire to "temper the rigor of justice with the oil of leniency," the pope authorized the archbishop to grant the absolutions, on condition that some other penance be assigned the offenders in lieu of a trip to Rome.[25] However, when the Archbishop of Lund expressed his reluctance to permit his servants to go to Rome for absolution from excommunication incurred by violence against clerics, the pope refused to mitigate the sentence unless the defendants actually were eager to set out for Rome in order to escape their ecclesiastical master.[26]

A troublesome complication arose in the diocese of St.

[24] *Ibid.*, cols. 200–201.   [25] *Ibid.*, cols. 726–27.
[26] *Ibid.*, col. 816.

Andrews, in Scotland, where individuals had taken holy orders while still under sentence of excommunication for violence against the clergy. When consulted by the bishop in regard to a case of this type, Innocent ruled that a distinction should be drawn between those who had unwittingly aggravated their guilt by accepting ordination in ignorance of the penalty incurred by their violence, and those who were fully aware of their status. Individuals ordained when they knew they were ineligible were to be degraded and permanently barred from ordination. The cases of others were reserved for the decision of the pope, who cautioned the prelate not to absolve them on his own initiative unless subsequent permission to do so was received from Rome. In the event the offenders had taken monastic vows while excommunicated for violence against churchmen, their abbots were empowered to absolve them unless their attacks on clerics had entailed effusion of blood, loss of a member, or mutilation. In such cases, or if the offense had been committed against a bishop, abbot, or ecclesiastical personage of even greater dignity, papal absolution at Rome was requisite.[27]

Innocent was equally energetic in seconding efforts of local ecclesiastical authorities to protect the property of the Church against lay spoliation. In a number of instances the seizure of the lands and goods of the Church was incident to the civil wars in Sicily and Germany, and the pope's intervention, therefore, was dictated not only by his solicitude for the preservation of ecclesiastical liberties but also by his unflagging determination to ensure the triumph of major policies.

The efforts of Markwald of Anweiler to gain control of

[27] *Ibid.*, CCXVI, cols. 1249–50.

the Sicilian kingdom after the death of Henry VI were accompanied by a number of infringements of ecclesiastical property rights. Innocent declared that he "bore these outrages with patience, for, just as the tares are not gathered and bundled for burning until after the harvest, so [he] was bound to tolerate evil until it was necessary to impose sentence." Finally, however, the pope announced that Markwald had actually committed sundry outrages in the sight of papal legates, who thereupon had excommunicated him. Innocent approved the sentence and ordered it publicly proclaimed. The pontiff furthermore absolved from their oaths all who had sworn to support Markwald, since oaths to a prince "who opposes God and His Saints and tramples upon Their precepts" were not binding.[28] Nevertheless, Markwald remained unchastened by papal wrath, and continued his depredations until his death in 1202.[29]

Civil war in Germany likewise engendered confiscation and spoliation. Philip of Swabia was charged with seizing properties of the Bishop of Würzburg, as well as those of his suffragans and relatives. The pope ordered the excommunication of the Hohenstaufen prince and the interdiction of his lands if his aggressions did not immediately cease, but the subsequent murder of the bishop, for which Philip was not personally blamed, overshadowed the property seizures.[30]

After the assassination of Philip, in 1208, partisans of his former rival, Otto of Brunswick (Otto IV), seized the properties of Bishop Eckbert of Bamberg. Innocent author-

[28] *Ibid.*, CCXIV, cols. 34–35.
[29] "Gesta," in Migne (ed.), *P.L.*, CCXIV, cols. liii, lvi–lxii.
[30] *Supra*, 4–5.

ized two legates to investigate the case, since charges of a
grave nature had been lodged against the bishop by Otto's
adherents. In the event the charges were sustained, the
legates were authorized to depose the prelate and to deprive him of all benefices; otherwise, if he successfully performed canonical purgation, he was to be acquitted, and
the confiscated properties were to be returned. The legates
were unable to proceed, however, since the bishop's accusers
announced their intention of appealing to Rome.

The bishop appeared at Rome within the stipulated time,
but his accusers, although in the city to attend Otto's coronation, made no effort to secure a hearing of the case. The
pope stated that he would have been perfectly justified in
rendering a verdict in favor of the bishop by default, but
in his "abundance of caution" he recommitted the case to
the Archbishop of Mainz, the Bishop of Würzburg, and
the Abbot of Fulda. These dignitaries were ordered to
procure the restoration of the properties of the Bamberg
diocese, unless the charges against the bishop should even
yet be sustained.[31] Since the Duke of Austria had apparently
taken some of the Bamberg properties, the Archbishop of
Salzburg was directed to warn him to restore them at once,
together with all incomes received during the illicit tenure.[32] Excommunication and interdict of his lands were
threatened in the event of noncompliance.[33]

In 1202 the Bishop of Meissen complained that the
Count of Witin prevented his vassals from paying tithes in
that diocese and aggravated his offense by interfering with
the archdeacon when he attempted to exercise legitimate
jurisdiction in fiefs possessed by the count. The Archbishop

[31] Migne (ed.), *P.L.*, CCXVI, cols. 149–50.
[32] *Ibid.*, cols. 150–51.   [33] *Ibid.*, col. 151.

of Magdeburg was accordingly ordered by Innocent to impose ecclesiastical censures to force the count to desist from his aggressions. Witnesses who refused to testify against the count because of favor or fear likewise were declared amenable to such censures if they persisted in their failure to give evidence. The archbishop was also directed to halt the building of a castle on the lands of the Meissen diocese by the Burgrave of Donyn.[34]

Innocent had several encounters with the English monarchy prior to the famous controversy incident to the installation of Stephen Langton as Archbishop of Canterbury. In a letter to King Richard, written in January, 1198, the pope expressed great sadness because the king hearkened to the counsels of the wicked and frustrated the efforts the pontiff was making in behalf of the monarchy. The prior and monks of Canterbury complained that the king had ordered their treasures inventoried and sealed with royal and archiepiscopal seals without provision for the imposition of the chapter seal. Alarmed lest this pointed exclusion should betoken an attempt to deprive them of their rights, the monks had protested, only to suffer confiscation of their properties in reprisal. The pope, complaining that an old grievance which he had hoped was dead and buried now was resurrected, ordered the king to restore everything to its status prior to the issue of the royal decrees.[35]

John's offenses were more serious. On one occasion he sent the Bishop of Bath and several pledged crusaders to Innocent III with certain requests. Innocent declared that he was unable to grant all the king's desires; consequently,

---

[34] Gersdorf and von Posern-Klett (eds.), *Codex dipl. Saxoniae*, II, 66–67, 73–74.

[35] Migne (ed.), *P.L.*, CCXIV, col. 451.

when the emissaries returned to England, John persecuted them and despoiled them of their properties. In his exasperation at the pope's failure to comply with his requests, John also ordered that henceforth no heed should be paid to the mandates of the papal legates, a harbinger of the policy he was to adopt in the Langton controversy. Fortunately, the pope declared, the errant king rescinded this order, an order the like of which no other Christian prince had dared to issue. But aside from his abuse of the Bishop of Bath and his diplomatic associates, the king was oppressing the Bishop of Poitiers and impeding elections to vacant prelacies so that he might continue to enjoy the revenues, particularly in the See of Lincoln. The king, exhorted to honor the Roman Church and to desist from his contumacy, was ordered to make prompt amends for his offenses.[36]

John's oppression of the Bishop of Limoges also stirred the pontiff's indignation. The king had seized manors and other episcopal possessions, even offerings dedicated to the saints; he had also imposed illegal exactions on the diocesan clergy. "If only the king would realize how much harm and sadness he inflicted upon the whole Church by his conduct," the pope complained, aside from the anxiety occasioned at Rome by such irreverent and ignominious treatment of bishops. Should the pope refrain from taking action, his own conscience would accuse him; and he, therefore, ordered John immediately to restore all the bishop's possessions if he wished to avoid an interdict on his kingdom.[37]

Seizure of church properties by laymen was virtually inevitable as a result of the creation of the Latin Kingdom of Constantinople by the ill-fated Fourth Crusade and the

[36] *Ibid.*, cols. 1175–77. [37] *Ibid.*, col. 1036.

consequent partial transition of the Greek Church to Roman Catholic control. The archbishopric of Larissa was a frequent sufferer from spoliation. In one instance, the metropolitan and his suffragans complained that the Constable of Romania, the imperial bailiff, and other laymen had seized monasteries and other properties in his province, claiming the right of advowson (*jus patronatus*). Laymen accordingly were refusing to pay tithes to ecclesiastical institutions thus affected, in view of their illegal tenure, and the pope ordered immediate restitution.[38]

The Countess of Montferrat also enriched herself at the expense of the Larissan archdiocese, despite the admonitions of the metropolitans of Athens and Thebes. The pope ordered that she be compelled to give up the properties she had seized on pain of ecclesiastical censures.[39] She was also compelled to give up properties belonging to the chapter of the Cathedral of St. Sophia of Constantinople.[40] In 1210, the emperor himself was ordered to permit the Archbishop of Larissa to regain what rightfully belonged to him.[41]

In another case, the Bishop of Gardiki, in Thessaly, complained that three days after his consecration he was compelled to leave his diocese on business. He entrusted the management of certain properties during his absence to the Constable of the Kingdom of Thessalonike, later called the Constable of Romania, but this lay official refused to return the properties, even three years after the bishop had made formal request for their restitution. As a result of the constable's recalcitrance, the diocese was reduced to such

[38] *Ibid.*, CCXVI, cols. 298, 301. [39] *Ibid.*, col. 299.
[40] *Ibid.*, cols. 456–57. See also *ibid.*, cols. 302–303; CCXV, col. 1467.
[41] *Ibid.*, CCXVI, cols. 297–98. See *ibid.*, cols. 470, 597, 612 for similar cases.

penury that only three clerks could be supported by its income. Innocent, in letters of July 14, 1208, and July 5, 1210, ordered the return of the illicitly held property.[42] At the time he wrote the second letter he also directed the constable to make similar restitution to the diocese of Cardica, which he had despoiled, "lest the Lord Christ, provoked by his sins, arise against him and deprive him of far more than he gained by his disobedience." [43]

Antelmus, Archbishop of Patras, also had reason to bemoan the aggressions of powerful laymen. In 1210 the Lord of Achaia "and certain other Latins having temporal dominion in this land seized possessions which the Church was accustomed to hold in Greek times." Violence was employed against the clergy in connection with their spoliation, and according to *post facto* laws issued by the lay powers concerned, the aggrieved clerics were required to sue for redress in secular courts. More and more ecclesiastical business was being drawn into lay courts, where anything decided in favor of clerical suitors was ignored. Lay investiture, refusal to pay tithes, prolonged vacancies in benefices, and open consorting with excommunicated persons were other palpable offenses of the lay oppressors of the Church, according to the archbishop's complaint. Innocent, in reply, ordered the Archbishop of Larissa to compel the temporal lords concerned to desist from their outrageous practices.[44]

Papal assistance was again forthcoming to enable the Archbishop of Patras to save the Church of St. Theodore.

[42] *Ibid.*, CCXV, cols. 1434–35; CCXVI, cols. 299–300. For identification, see P. B. Gams, *Series episcoporum ecclesiae Catholicae* (Leipzig, 1931), 432.
[43] Migne (ed.), *P.L.*, CCXVI, cols. 300–301. See also *ibid.*, cols. 222, 230–31, 582.
[44] *Ibid.*, cols. 338–39.

As the prelate informed the pope, this old cathedral had been the site of the enthronement of archbishops from earliest times, and in its crypt had been interred the remains of the metropolitans who had served the see. Now, however, the city had grown up around the church to such an extent that it was necessary for the archbishop to move from the cathedral, and the bones of his predecessors were exhumed in order to make way for new secular construction. Innocent ordered the Archbishop of Larissa to see that the archbishop was restored to his traditional place, and that sufficient vacant space around the cathedral was assured to prevent further interference with ecclesiastical functions or sepulture.[45]

Some financial relief also was secured for the archbishopric of Patras. Henry, ruler of the Latin Kingdom of Constantinople, had established a new monastery in the city, dedicating to it twenty-five pounds of pepper yearly, which he ordinarily received from archiepiscopal revenues. When it became difficult for the archbishopric to pay this amount, however, it was reduced by half, and ultimately to five pounds per year. Then, after the church was despoiled of many of its possessions, it became difficult to pay even the five pounds. The pope accordingly authorized the Archbishop of Larissa to make whatever adjustment would be necessary, dependent, of course, upon the prelate's success in carrying out the pope's mandate to enforce the restoration of the Patras properties.[46]

Aggressions against Manfred, Archbishop of Durazzo, reflected lay opposition to his installation. The prelate informed Innocent that he had been properly elected by the canons who had suffragan rights, and his election was con-

[45] *Ibid.*, col. 340.   [46] *Ibid.*, col. 339.

firmed by the Patriarch of Constantinople, who thereupon consecrated him. The Venetian rector, who held the properties of the cathedral church during the vacancy, refused to give them up and even prevented the duly consecrated archbishop from entering the city to assume his duties. On one occasion the prelate did succeed in entering the city incognito, but upon subsequent identification the rector ordered him forcibly expelled. Appeals to the Venetian doge and his counselors were unavailing, since the secular officials claimed that no archbishop could be elected to the see without their consent.

Since the Venetian action was "in prejudice of the liberty of the Church," Innocent hastened to command the bishops of Padua and Ceneda, acting as his legates, to order the doge to permit the installation of the archbishop, as well as to order his rector to surrender the ecclesiastical property he was illegally holding.[47] In a letter to the doge himself, the pope declared, "If you acknowledge yourself to be in the service of Him who adopts His servants as sons and crowns them as king, it will behoove you not to offend His spouse who stands at His right hand in shining garments." The Venetian ruler was admonished to permit the aggrieved archbishop to hold his possessions in peace and to see to it that he was suitably indemnified for losses sustained since his election.[48]

The church of Corinth suffered from the confiscations of Godfrey of Villehardouin. The pope reminded this powerful prince that "God had filled his hands magnificently," and for the sake of the reverence he owed to St. Peter and the papacy, he was admonished to return the possessions at once. Protection of the Corinthian church

[47] *Ibid.*, cols. 105–106.　　　　[48] *Ibid.*, cols. 106–107.

would redound greatly to Godfrey's credit, the pope declared, but if he failed to mend his ways and show an example to others, the Archbishop of Thebes and other prelates were authorized to invoke ecclesiastical censures against him.[49]

Several communes of northern Italy, long a thorn in the side of the papacy, were subjected to censure for infringement of the property rights of the Church. In writing to the podesta and populace of the city of Urbino, Innocent declared that he had countenanced their insolence, expecting that clemency would induce repentance for the wrongs inflicted upon the Church. Instead, the citizenry had become more obstreperous, until their sins were even graver than their earlier offenses. As a culmination to their outrages they stole church property "before the pope's own eyes." Innocent ordered restoration of this property within twenty-five days, upon pain of excommunication and interdict in the event of disobedience. If the city authorities failed to comply promptly with the pontiff's orders, they were also threatened with the imposition of a fine of 4,000 marks in addition to ecclesiastical penalties, so that "they would be more aware of the weight of apostolic displeasure." [50]

Another case involved merchants of Pisa. The Judge of Torres, in Sardinia, had taken an oath to the Pisans in which he promised to order execution of judgment against alleged debtors upon presentation of documentary evidence by Pisan creditors. Laymen, and even clergy, had been forced to settle alleged debts upon demand of the Pisans, with the result that not only were sums collected that were

---

[49] *Ibid.*, col. 590. For similar cases, see *ibid.*, cols. 302, 323–24, 594–95.
[50] *Ibid.*, col. 84.

not actually owed but in a number of instances the same debt was repaid by churchmen two or even three times. The judge was warned that neither he nor the Pisans could subject clergy to secular judgment, oath or no oath, and he was ordered to desist from his illegal practices "lest in trying to please the Pisans he offend God and the Holy See." [51]

In 1204 Innocent found it necessary to expostulate with the judge because of his general interference with the clerical courts and his disposition to flout benefit of clergy. Natural law, the pope declared, forbade one from doing to others what he would not want done to himself. In effect, the judge was committing an offense against Divine Law by a transgression that even the law of man would prohibit, the pope continued. The judge has usurped clerical jurisdiction; yet he would be bitterly resentful if anyone attempted to infringe upon his own legal prerogatives, thus meting out with a different measure from that he himself would want used in meting out to him. To be sure, the pope went on, some clergy defamed themselves, but their status was not changed by their derelictions, and consequently they were answerable to ecclesiastical courts, just as the judge's retainers were held to account to him. Yet the judge, oblivious to considerations of law and equity,

---

[51] *Ibid.*, CCXV, col. 31. In another case Innocent declared that the Archbishop of Sassari, in Sardinia, was not bound to pay debts incurred by a predecessor unless payment would redound to the advantage of the Church. *Ibid.*, col. 430. The authorities of Cremona were excommunicated for attempting to tallage the clergy of that city. August Theiner (ed.), *Vetera monumenta Slavorum meridionalium historiam illustrantia*, 2 vols. (Rome, 1863), I, 61. The King of Sweden also had to be reminded that clergy could not be brought before secular courts. J. G. Liljegren (ed.), *Svenskt Diplomatarium*, 5 vols. in 8 (Stockholm, 1829–1867), I, 154. For other cases of attempts to extort payments from the clergy see August Potthast (ed.), *Regesta Pontificum Romanorum*, 2 vols. (Berlin, 1875), I, Nos. 3415, 3434, 4327, 4904.

was summoning clergy before his courts. Here judgments by ordeal were administered, although the clergy were not permitted to take part in such procedure. In assuming jurisdiction over the clergy, the judge in effect was presuming to judge the Lord Himself, Innocent maintained, in ordering immediate cessation of these practices.[52]

Interference with clerical immunity in civil courts in Matera evoked Innocent's declaration that the "immunity of the clerical order is sealed by the privilege of liberty, since it has its judges before whom it can and should be summoned and is completely exempt from secular judgment." The clergy were free from the burdens of civic responsibilities, the pope declared, in order that they might more freely fight for the Lord.[53] In a letter addressed to the people of Matera, written to accompany one sent to the aggrieved clergy, the pope reasoned that since they were rightly called sons of the Church, the people were also its servants. The Church, their mother, was the servant of God; inasmuch as servants inherited the status of their mother, the people were servants of the Church. Consequently, the practice of summoning clergy before secular courts was to cease immediately, and any sentences which ecclesiastical authorities might promulgate to enforce the rights of the clergy were assured of papal approval.[54]

In the diocese of Périgueux the pope's intervention was sought by the bishop to stop the laymen's practice of collecting tithes from the clergy. Innocent wrote that "since it is inappropriate and contrary to reason that laics, who are required to pay tithes to ecclesiastical persons, should presume to extort them from clergy in a preposterous in-

[52] Migne (ed.), *P.L.*, CCXV, cols. 394–95.
[53] *Ibid.*, CCXIV, col. 714.   [54] *Ibid.*, cols. 714–15.

version of the order of things," any such charges, no matter on what pretext levied, were void. Any laymen who invoked violence to flout the papal decretal were threatened with interdict.[55]

The Viscount of Melun and some clerical abettors seized lands, pastures, and tithes belonging to the monastery of St. Martin de Campis. The viscount also defrauded the monastery of the services of serfs subject to it. The pope, in response to an appeal from the aggrieved establishment, ordered the viscount to desist from his spoliations and commanded the serfs to show proper obedience to their ecclesiastical lords.[56]

An interesting case arose concerning a Cistercian house in the archdiocese of Tours. The house held certain properties with the stipulation that no tax should be paid on the products of the monks' labor or investment. Nevertheless, laymen were attempting to exact tithes, claiming that the immunities applied only to such lands as were lying fallow in any given year. The pope, in answer to the request of the monastery for aid, declared that such an interpretation of the immunities and exemptions of the establishment was "perverse and contrary to right reason," as well as being clearly incompatible with the language of the papal grant that had stipulated that the monastery was to pay no tithes of any sort to laymen. Excommunication of laymen attempting to extort such payments in the future was threatened, and clergy who abetted them in such efforts were liable to suspension.[57]

[55] *Ibid.*, cols. 433–34.

[56] Saint-Rene Taillandier, *Histoire du château et du bourg de Blandy* (Paris, 1854), 159–60.

[57] Geslin and de Barthelemy, *Anciens evêches de Bretagne*, IV, 56–57. For a similar case in which the same lay interpretation of monastic im-

The city of Parma incurred the pope's anger as a result of the robbery of one of his legates. Both the legate's private funds and sums belonging to the pope were stolen, and although the bishop, consul, and other civil dignitaries had restored part of the money, their promise to repay the remainder was not fulfilled. The partial settlement nonetheless induced the legate to relax the sentences of excommunication and interdict he had imposed on the city and its officials. Innocent declared that since it was the policy of the Holy See to be merciful to those who acknowledged the error of their ways, he was willing to waive repayment of the whole sum that had been stolen, provided those actually guilty of the theft were brought to justice.[58] When Simon de Montfort, leader of the Albigensian Crusade, was robbed of 5,000 marks sometime after the successful siege of Carcassonne, the pope was not so indulgent. He ordered strict enforcement of the sentences of excommunication that had been promulgated against those in any way implicated in the robbery.[59]

Many cases occurred where laymen claimed the *jus patronatus* giving them the right to present candidates for vacant benefices. Disputes as to the validity of such rights naturally arose, most of which, if submitted to the papacy, were handled in a routine manner. Occasionally, however, allegations of fraud were so grave as to necessitate a papal pronouncement of a more general character. In the diocese of Winchester, for example, laymen with the *jus patronatus*

---

munities was involved, see Angelo Manrique (ed.), *Cisterciensium seu verius ecclesiasticorum annalium a condito Cistercio*, 4 vols. (Lyons, 1642–1659), III, 438.

[58] Migne (ed.), *P.L.*, CCXIV, col. 372.

[59] Martin Bouquet (ed.), *Recueil des historiens des Gaules et de la France*, 24 vols. (Paris, 1900–1904), XIX, 525.

had devised an ingenious scheme to retain the income of the benefices themselves. When a vacancy occurred they granted the benefice to a relative, with a merely nominal stipend, such as a pound of pepper or wax per year, or an annual monetary payment of one bezant. The remainder of the incomes the patrons kept for themselves. They even arranged that this corrupt practice could be continued after their demises by providing in their wills that their heirs should continue to fill the benefices by paying only nominal stipends to the incumbents. Needless to say, Innocent ordered the practice stopped as soon as it was brought to his attention.[60]

SUPPRESSION OF CLERICAL VIOLENCE

Some realization of the magnitude of the task that confronted reformers zealous to improve the morality of the ecclesiastical personnel can be gleaned from cases of violence by clerics that necessitated invocation of the disciplinary powers of the Holy See.[61] One case that aroused widespread indignation occurred in the archdiocese of Tours. Several canons of evil reputation hired four brigands to waylay and kill the Abbot of Cellini. In return for payment of £60 by the canons, the assassins murdered the abbot while he was on his way to Matins. The murderers were captured, and their confessions subsequently confirmed the guilt of the clergy, already attested by the evidence of reputable witnesses. There was considerable local demand

---

[60] Migne (ed.), *P.L.*, CCXV, col. 724.

[61] According to Stephen of Tournai almost every case of clerical misconduct aroused eventual papal action. Selmar Scheler, *Sitten und Bildung der französischen Geistlichkeit nach den Briefen Stephans von Tournai* (Berlin, 1915), 61.

that the canons should be surrendered to secular authorities for capital punishment; but advisers of the archbishop, to whom the case was submitted, held that they were amenable only to ecclesiastical jurisdiction.

The prelate finally sought Innocent's advice as to the proper procedure. He ordered that the guilty canons be degraded from orders and imprisoned for life in solitary confinement on bread and water. But if public anger remained unabated, the archbishop was directed to relax the offenders to the secular authorities for the infliction of the death penalty. During the investigation of the case it was reported to the pope that all the canons of the chapter were guilty of contumacy, and many had committed grave offenses. Innocent therefore ordered that if these charges were true, the canons should be replaced by monks of another order and sent to strict monasteries for correction.[62]

Another instance that occasioned papal intervention resulted from the sacrilegious conduct of a minor deacon and a chaplain of Rouen. On several occasions the defendants laid violent hands on clerical colleagues of their diocese, and they also were charged with seizure of sacred vessels and vestments. They interfered with church services by their outrageous deportment and on one occasion went to the length of hurling several corpses into a church. The deacon, aside from his other offenses, was charged with kicking a woman, with whom he had had illicit relations, so severely as to cause an abortion. The pope, after careful study of the case, ordered the suspension and excommunication of the guilty clerics.[63]

Another notorious incident occurred in the diocese of

[62] Migne (ed.), *P.L.*, CCXVI, cols. 318–20.
[63] *Ibid.*, CCXIV, col. 181.

Verona. An archpriest was waylaid and murdered by a cleric who long had cherished a grudge against him. The victim was "a man of good repute, generous, a lover of religion, a cultivator of hospitality and other works of piety," but his assassin already had incurred excommunication for carrying arms and consorting with iniquitous men.

The guilty cleric was imprisoned, and there was considerable local sentiment for his relaxation to the secular arm. But the Podesta of Verona decided that the homicide should be considered the result of a duel, and the defendant and his father paid £800 to relatives of the victim in order to settle the case. Not content with saving the defendant from capital punishment, his relatives and friends then attempted to have the sentence of excommunication lifted and his benefices restored. This phase of the case finally came to the attention of Innocent, who indignantly replied that the deprivation of benefices was permanent. He also ordered that the excommunication of the offender be publicly proclaimed without hope of appeal unless the bishop should report that suitable penance had been performed.[64]

Equally severe punishment was ordered by the pope in the case of an archdeacon of Lyons who had been convicted of highway robbery. He had held up both clerical and lay travelers and stolen their belongings, and he apparently richly deserved the excommunication and deprivation inflicted upon him.[65]

In the notorious case of Maurice de Blason, Bishop of Poitiers, the prelate's violent acts were aggravated by the riotous conduct of his retainers. When complaints arose against the bishop, the pope gave instructions to the prior of a monastery located in the diocese to make an investiga-

[64] *Ibid.,* col. 464. [65] *Ibid.,* col. 1090.

tion. The bishop thereupon "conceived a violent hatred against the prior and inflicted pain on the pope in the person of his representative." A relative of the bishop, abetted by bailiffs of the Castle of Mirabello, refused to permit the tillage of the prior's lands. The bishop's servants, emboldened by their master's example, stole grapes from the prior's vineyards before they were ripe and drove away the prior's serfs when they attempted to save the rest of the crop. In the brawling that ensued, clergy were flogged and divested of their clothing by the rampaging retainers of the bishop without a word or gesture from him to restrain their excesses. As the violence continued, the bishop's servants tore down a valuable house in the legitimate possession of the prior and used stone and timber salvaged from the wreckage to strengthen the fortifications of the Mirabello castle. When the aggrieved prior courageously appeared in the bishop's court to bring charges against his persecutors, the prelate admitted his responsibility for the outrages and agreed to pay damages. This agreement was flouted, however, and when the prior ventured to complain, the bishop declared that "he was pope in his diocese."

Innocent personally pronounced the sentence of excommunication against the offending bishop and ordered his suspension from office. In the event he dared celebrate while under the ban, the pope declared he would be permanently degraded from orders. The bishop yielded, however, obviating the necessity for such severity.[66]

In 1207 an uproar was created throughout the diocese of Poitiers by Hilary, former abbot of the monastery of Burguol who had been deposed for misconduct. After his deposition Hilary seized possession of the monastery and

[66] *Ibid.*, CCXVI, cols. 795–98.

attempted illegally to collect its revenues, while monks of the house were subjected to contumely and dunned for payment of debts contracted in their name by their former superior. The monks feared to venture outside their cloister, as the renegade threatened to kill or dismember them, and they knew he would shrink from nothing. Matters came to a head one night when abettors of the former abbot burned a barn belonging to the monastery, and it was alleged that only an opportune shift of the wind saved the entire monastery from destruction.[67]

When Innocent was apprized of the facts in the case, he ordered the offender confined in another monastery for the performance of penance, with excommunication automatically incurred if he ventured to leave.[68] All directly involved in the incendiarism were excommunicated, along with those who attempted to burden the aggrieved monastery by false debts.[69] Monks of the establishment who were known to be supporters of Hilary were ordered chastised in accordance with the degree of their involvement in his scandalous actions.[70]

Disputes over the occupancy of benefices were a fertile cause of violence, as forcible means were employed by clerics to assume or defend possession of them. In one instance the abbot of a monastery in the diocese of Perigord forcibly seized a chapel from a canon to whom it had been assigned, and resisted all efforts to expel him. Even a sentence of excommunication imposed by the bishop failed to daunt him, so that it was necessary for the pope to threaten the imposition of ecclesiastical censures to reduce him to obedience.[71]

[67] *Ibid.*, CCXV, cols. 1118–19.   [68] *Ibid.*
[69] *Ibid.*, cols. 1120–21.   [70] *Ibid.*, col. 1121.   [71] *Ibid.*, col. 298.

31

On another occasion an unseemly altercation between the Abbot of St. Augustine and the Archdeacon of Canterbury concerning the tenure of a benefice became so heated that the archdeacon smashed an altar, broke a chalice, and tore vestments belonging to the monastery. The pope committed the vexatious dispute to the Bishop of London and the Abbot of St. Edmund's, with powers to determine the disposition of the benefice; but the archdeacon was directed to make suitable atonement for the damage he had caused, as a necessary prerequisite to the settlement of the case.[72]

Exceptionally violent treatment was the portion of the priest of St. Christopher's of Auxerre, who ventured to complain that the prior of the monastery of Auxerre was taking an excessively large portion of the income of the parish. The prior's initial reaction was to have the priest boycotted so that no tradesmen would do business with him. In these circumstances it soon became impossible for the priest to maintain residence in his manse, and he was driven to the expedient of living in his church, shunned by parishioners because of their fear of the prior and monks.

On All Saints' Day, 1211, when the virtually besieged priest ventured forth to secure desperately needed supplies, he was pelted with stones and forced to scurry back into the church. On Christmas, the hapless clerk underwent worse indignities when servants of the prior caught him outside his sanctuary and thrashed him so severely that his hearing was permanently impaired. Beaten into semiconsciousness, he was taken before the prior and forced to swear to refrain from further proceedings in regard to the parish revenues.

William Seignelay, Bishop of Auxerre, then imposed an

[72] *Ibid.*, cols. 733-34.

interdict on the church and ordered a trial. But the prior managed to secure a change of venue, of which the priest was not informed, so that he had the expense and fatigue of a journey for nothing. With his church closed and his meager resources dissipated, the unfortunate cleric was reduced to begging, but the prior still refused redress for the injuries he had inflicted. When the bishop at last excommunicated the prior to force a satisfactory settlement, the latter managed to get the sentence revoked without a hearing and celebrated Divine Office while the interdict imposed because of the beating of the priest still was in effect.

When the pope's attention was finally secured by the appeals of both parties, he ordered reaffirmation of the previous sentences against the prior. If the offender had ventured to celebrate while under excommunication or in defiance of an interdict, he was to be suspended and sent to Rome to seek absolution. The priest was reimbursed for the expense and damages he had incurred, but the pope issued no directions as to apportionment of the revenues which had been the original issue between priest and prior. In all probability, the £10 Paris per year, which previously appointed commissioners in the diocese of Troyes had awarded to the priest out of the income of his parish, was finally obtained.[73]

A number of cases in which clergy were involved in violence resulted from accidental circumstances, and strict application of the Canon Law would have been inequitable. In one instance a clergyman testified that while a student at the University of Bologna he had gone to the room of a schoolfellow to study. Good-natured banter between the two students ultimately led to an impromptu wrestling

[73] *Ibid.*, CCXVI, cols. 631–33.

match, during which the appellant grasped his adversary firmly by the head. The latter slipped this hold and, in doing so, fell against a wall and fractured a shinbone. Complications ensued, and the injured student died fourteen days later, not without suspicion that his death was attributable to the negligence of the attending physician. The cleric thus presumably guilty of involuntary homicide performed the penance assigned by the Bishop of Freising and, upon appeal to Innocent, was permitted to retain his order and eligibility for promotion.[74]

A priest of Sens reported to the pontiff an equally tragic mishap. While passing some boys who were shooting arrows at a target, he accepted an invitation to join in the sport. His hand slipped as he aimed the bow; and the arrow, taking an erratic course, struck one of the boys in the head. The victim of the accident died a few days later, and the grief-stricken priest reported the affair to the Archbishop and Archdeacon of Sens. The archdeacon, impressed by the priest's genuine contrition, permitted him to hold his benefice; and Innocent, when the case was submitted to him, confirmed this decision.[75]

Bishop Roderic of Siguenza was involved in an affair that graphically illustrated the turbulence of the age. While Mass was being said, a multitude of parishioners filled the cathedral, and eventually pressed into the choir and crowded about the altar. The bishop ordered the canons to restore some semblance of decorum, but their importunities were fruitless. The prelate then lost his temper and, seizing a cane, drove back the crowd, prodding some and lightly striking others. The canons joined in belaboring the disrespectful laymen, and in the ensuing melee

[74] *Ibid.*, cols. 30–31.   [75] *Ibid.*, CCXIV, col. 169.

a youth was struck on the head. For a month the victim appeared healthy, eating and drinking normally and engaging in hard manual labor. Then he was advised to submit to an operation upon his injured head; and an old, unskilled doctor made an incision into his skull. Four days after the operation the patient died—according to the testimony of four physicians, as the result of clumsy surgery.

Public clamor arose against the bishop, who was charged with having caused the youth's death by a blow with his cane. He accordingly abstained from celebrating divine offices; and the pope, to whom the case was explained, ordered an investigation. After careful examination of all the canons and the only witness who claimed to have actually seen the bishop deliver the blow, the prelate's accusers were ordered to withdraw their charges. The pope, who received a report of the investigation and the testimony of reputable doctors, declared that the bishop was guiltless and directed that the verdict of the physicians be publicly proclaimed.[76]

Interesting legal issues were raised by the case of the chaplain of the monastery of Holy Trinity of Maloleone. A criminal entered the abbey chapel and stole a chalice, several altar ornaments, and ecclesiastical books. The chaplain caught the culprit making off with his booty and struck the fleeing "son of iniquity" with a mattock. Parishioners in the neighborhood were aroused by the chaplain's cries and eventually overtook the thief, whom they fell upon and killed with swords and clubs.

The chaplain was sorely troubled by the fear that the blow he had struck might have resulted in the death of the thief, even if additional injuries had not been inflicted. A

[76] *Ibid.*, CCXVI, cols. 160–62.

year after the event he revealed his story to the abbot, who subsequently besought the pope to exercise clemency in the case.

Innocent declared that when four or five persons were involved in a brawl against one person who was mortally wounded, the assailant who actually struck the fatal blow was guilty of homicide. In view of the precedents, the pope directed that the following questions be asked: First, did the chaplain strike a lethal blow; that is, would the death of the thief have ensued even though no additional wounds had been inflicted? Did he have the intent to kill the culprit when he caught him in his sacrilegious act? Was the wound inflicted with the mattock so light that in the judgment of expert physicians it would not ordinarily cause death? The pope declared that effort also should be made to ascertain if the parishioners had struck the thief at the chaplain's instigation.

If it could be proved that the chaplain had not struck a fatal blow, he was authorized to officiate. On the other hand, if this could not be ascertained, he was ordered to abstain, since, according to the pontiff, it was better to err on the side of caution, in view of the enormity of the sin that would be committed if he officiated with bloodguilt on his conscience.

If it could be shown that the priest had struck in self-defense, he should be considered blameless, since civil, as well as canon, law recognized self-defense as an extenuating circumstance. Yet a blow struck in self-defense should be moderate and in no wise aggravated in severity by a desire for vengeance, however fleeting. A plea of self-defense in this case was difficult to entertain, for, as Innocent pointed out, a mattock was not the type of instrument that ordinarily would make a minor wound; and the likelihood of superficial injury was further reduced by the fact that the victim had been struck on the head. In view of these circumstances, the pope decided that the chaplain would have to abstain from the altar unless it could be unequivocally shown that his blow could not have occasioned more than minor injury.[77]

In some instances, cases referred to the pope involved only the question of indirect guilt of the clergy. For example, a deacon in the diocese of Huesca was granted a benefice which an abbot illegally seized and refused to surrender, despite the importunities of the deacon and his relatives. One evening the deacon supped with a group of relatives and friends, and during the meal was assured that efforts would be made to avenge his grievances. He pleaded that nothing be done that would jeopardize his tenure of Holy Orders, however, and specifically demanded that there be no further talk of killing the abbot. Nevertheless, the relatives killed the abbot; and the deacon, fearing that he had incurred guilt, refrained from participation in divine service. The case ultimately came to the attention of the pope, who directed that the deacon be declared eligible for ordination as a priest if the facts as represented to the Holy See could be substantiated. The pontiff took occasion to remark that a good man frequently felt a sense of guilt when he actually was blameless, and that the deacon was to be commended for his fine sensibilities.[78]

On occasion, malicious accusations involved clergy in serious difficulties. When the church of Puy needed a priest, the bishop announced his decision to ordain a cantor of this church, a man of outstanding learning and presumably irreproachable morality. However, a woman of the parish charged that the cantor had kicked her so severely as to

[77] *Ibid.*, cols. 64–65.   [78] *Ibid.*, cols. 1253–54.

induce an abortion. The cantor therefore refused to accept ordination while under this suspicion. He admitted that a long time before, while on a picnic, he had kicked a woman during a playful scuffle. He doubted that this was the woman who now accused him; and he insisted that, in any event, he had not kicked anyone hard enough to cause a serious injury.

The bishop took the complainant to her confessor to ascertain the truth, but nothing was learned to clarify the facts of the case. The prelate believed her story untrue and invented to extort money. The pope, whose advice was sought by the bishop, directed that the cantor be ordained, as originally planned, if there seemed to be sufficient reason to discredit the charges against him.[79] The final outcome of the case cannot be learned, since no further correspondence appears in the papal registers. But there is reason to believe that even if the facts alleged by the woman were true, the cantor could have been absolved, for in a somewhat similar case Innocent permitted a priest to officiate, although he admitted having caused an abortion by violently tugging the girdle of a woman in an advanced stage of pregnancy.[80]

The cases gleaned from the papal letters were, to be sure, exceptional, as attested by the fact that they required the pontiff's attention. Nevertheless, exceptional as they indubitably were, they show that even after the Cistercian Reform the clergy still were occasionally involved in the turbulence of the age in which feudal lords were just beginning to yield grudging obedience to the rising power of monarchical governments.

[79] *Ibid.*, CCXV, col. 484.   [80] *Ibid.*, CCXVI, col. 469.

CHAPTER II

ILLICIT TENURE OF BENEFICES

SIMONY

THE DELIBERATE buying and selling of spiritual things is prohibited both by Divine Law and by the law of the Church.[1] Indeed, in order to avoid even the appearance of simoniacal practice, the Church, in its definition of *Simonia Juris Ecclesiastici*, goes beyond the Divine Law in the strictness of its concept of the offense.[2]

The term "simony" was derived from the story of Simon Magus as told in Acts 8:18–21, and was first used officially, in the form of the adjective "simoniacal," by Pope Pelagius I (555–560).[3] Condemnation of Paul of Samosata in 268 A.D. was the first recorded instance of the action of the Church against simony, while the earliest extant legislation is a canon of the Synod of Elvira (306).[4] The Council of Chalcedon, in 452, strongly condemned both sale and purchase of clerical orders, a form of simony that had become increasingly prevalent after the triumph of the Church in its struggle with the Roman Empire.[5]

---

[1] W. A. Weber, *A History of Simony in the Christian Church* (Baltimore, 1909), 5; J. W. Richardson, *The Just Title in Canon 730* (Rome, 1936), 1.

[2] Weber, *History of Simony*, 5.

[3] L. M. Duchesne (ed.), *Liber Pontificalis*, 2 vols. (Paris, 1886–1892), I, 303.

[4] R. A. Ryder, *Simony, A Historical Synopsis and Commentary* (Washington, D.C., 1931), 6–7.

[5] Ryder, *Simony*, 8–9.

Feudalization of the Church in the ninth and tenth centuries multiplied the evils of simony, as traffic in benefices augmented the older abuses of extortion of fees and simoniacal bestowal of orders. To secure better enforcement of existent legislation, Nicholas I (858–867) drew distinctions in the gravity of the offense, while Clement II (1046–1047) stressed the intent in the transfer of benefices as a paramount factor in cases of alleged simony.[6] Leo IX (1049–1054) labored indefatigably to eradicate simony, as the great reform impulse of the tenth and eleventh centuries took increasing hold, and eventually the problem, from a practical standpoint, was merged in the great Investiture Struggle launched by the decrees of Gregory VII (1073–1086).[7]

By the time of the accession of Innocent III to the papal throne, the legislation of the Church against simony was virtually formulated. Innocent added little to existent canonical prohibitions; indeed, only one of his decretals is cited in the *Decretales Gregorii IX Papae*.[8] Yet, during his entire pontificate the pope was prompt to invoke the full rigor of the law against offenders, always, however, with the careful heed to equity that characterized his jurisprudence. Innocent was particularly concerned with procedural questions that arose in simony cases, especially when the guilt of the accused was established by the inquisitorial procedure which he was so largely instru-

---

[6] *Ibid.*, 22–23.

[7] Johannes Drehmann, *Papst Leo IX und die Simonie* (Leipzig and Berlin, 1908), *passim*.

[8] "Decretales Gregorii IX Papae," Lib. V, Tit. iii, cap. 34, in Aemilius Friedberg (ed.), *Corpus Juris Canonici*, 2 vols. (Leipzig, 1879–1881), II, col. 763. For summary of early legislation see "Decreti Secunda Pars," Causa I, quest. i, caps. 1–8, *ibid.*, I, cols. 357–59.

mental in devising as a means of purging the clergy of unworthy members.

Particularly reprehensible was the practice of extorting
money for the administration of the Sacraments or for the
performance of other religious services. Commercialization
of the means of salvation, the free gift of God, aside from
the illegality and obvious incongruity of the practice, in-
evitably engendered criticism among the laity and gave
point to the strictures of antisacerdotal groups.

Parishioners of Villa Franca, for example, complained
to Innocent that their chaplain extorted money for officiat-
ing at obsequies and for the blessing of infants. If the laity
refused such illegal payments, the chaplain cited alleged
impediments to preclude sepulture of the dead or the blessing of children. In response to this well-founded charge,
Innocent ordered the chaplain to desist from his simoniacal
practices and to make restitution of fees already exacted.[9]

Hugh of Auxerre, Bishop of St. Germain, refused the
Chrism and the Holy Oil unless payment was offered by the
recipient, according to charges brought against him in 1198
by the Abbot and convent of St. Germain of Auxerre. He
also refused to consecrate altars and churches or to admit
monks to Holy Orders without charge, in defiance of the
canons against simony. Innocent replied to these allegations by authorizing the abbot and monks to apply to any
other bishop for the desired ecclesiastical services if their
own bishop continued to impose financial exactions or delayed performance of his duties in the hope of receiving
money. The pope also declared that neither the accused
bishop nor any other prelate should demand money for
lifting a sentence of excommunication. If any member of

[9] Migne (ed.), *P.L.*, CCXIV, col. 191.

the monastic community had been subjected to a sentence of any kind for refusal to acquiesce in the bishop's simoniacal exactions, such sentence was *ipso facto* null and void.[10]

In July, 1199, Innocent wrote to Hubert Walter, Archbishop of Canterbury, in bitter condemnation of the simony prevalent among his suffragans. The pope declared that the Canterbury clergy, "their mouths watering for evil gains, were panting after simony under another name, saying in effect that by changing the name of the sin the guilt and punishment could be evaded." For a long time the Canterbury suffragans had been demanding money for the Holy Chrism, despite canonical prohibitions. In fear of punishment for their sin they moved forward the time of collection, accepting the payments in mid-Lent rather than after Easter, as though that would mitigate their guilt. Bishops of the province collected a silver mark for the investment of archdeacons, while deacons on such occasions demanded a white cow as an honorarium. If the candidate for investiture could not meet this bizarre requirement, he was permitted to pay a monetary fee, in a strategem obviously devised to extort money without openly requiring such payment. Innocent ordered the archbishop to eradicate these practices at once by invocation of all necessary disciplinary measures, lest the primate himself incur guilt by his remissness.[11]

Stephen Langton, shortly after his appointment (June 17, 1207) by Innocent to the archbishopric of Canterbury, sent a nuncio to the pope to report that simony was still raging in his province, particularly among the regular clergy. In view of the multitude of instances where "things had been received for a price which ought to be free," the archbishop hesitated to exercise severity and ac-

[10] *Ibid.*   [11] *Ibid.*, col. 657.

cordingly asked the pope's advice as to how to proceed.

Innocent replied that if the offenses were proved before the archbishop by the procedure of accusation, that is, with the charges submitted in writing and the accusers prepared to incur the risk of punishment (*lex talionis*) in the event they could not sustain their accusations, the greatest severity should be exercised. If inquisitorial procedure, initiated by the archbishop, was utilized to adduce proofs of the crimes, the guilty clergy should be deprived of their benefices and sent to strict monasteries or convents to do penance. Prelates against whom charges of simony were thus sustained were to be suspended from orders until completion of their penance. The archbishop was admonished to do all in his power to purge his province, with his authority supported by the pope. Sentences of excommunication and anathema were authorized whenever necessary to secure compliance with the reform measures.[12]

Another case involving extortion of fees for installation in clerical offices arose in the diocese of Paris. The Archdeacon of Paris attempted to collect 100 Parisian solidos as the price of installing an abbot and, indeed, wished to make payment of this sum a precedent for the collection of an annual charge on the monastery in like amount. Upon complaint of the aggrieved monastery, Innocent declared this exaction "contrary to reason and inimical to the institutes of the Holy Fathers" and strictly prohibited any such arrangements.[13]

In the case of the Archbishop of Besançon, Innocent directly ordered utilization of the inquisitorial procedure. The prelate was accused of grave sins, including concubinage and fornication, and the difficulty of securing evi-

---

[12] *Ibid.*, cols. 1231–32.   [13] *Ibid.*, CCXVI, col. 504.

dence by the *accusatio* procedure may have accounted for the pope's decision. The archbishop was also accused of simony, since he allegedly had accepted money for the bestowal of a deaconry. It was further charged that he had permitted monks and nuns to return to the world and even to marry. Priests and clergy were so vexed by the archbishop's extortions that "depressed by the burden of poverty they went about like peasants to the degradation of ecclesiastical honesty." Clerics had been killed in the prelate's own house, and no effort was made to punish those guilty of the crime, although their identities were known. Incendiaries were absolved by the archbishop for pecuniary considerations, and pledges were taken from the laity which the archbishop subsequently refused to return when properly redeemed. It was further charged that the archbishop had refused to ordain properly qualified candidates for the priesthood unless they first bound themselves by oath not to seek benefices in the province. The prelate moreover allegedly left his province for extended periods, and on the days of the great feasts, "when he should have honored the Church by his presence," he usually was absent.[14]

The inquisition ordered by the pope was directed to inquire into the charge of simony as well as into the other alleged derelictions of the prelate. Then, in May, 1213, Innocent ordered the Bishop of Langres and the Abbot of Morimond to depose the archbishop unless he could acquit himself with compurgation of three bishops or abbots.[15] Although no mention was made of the matter, the accused archbishop had been a supporter of Philip of Swabia in the great German civil war, and this factor may have had a

[14] *Ibid.*, cols. 479–81. [15] *Ibid.*, col. 866.

bearing on Innocent's insistence that the case be rigorously and successfully prosecuted.[16]

Bishop Godfrey of Coventry also was the recipient of the special attention of the Holy See. Innocent declared that surely the prelate realized "how odious the sin of simony was to God and how much evil followed from it." Yet many clerics in the diocese held benefices as a result of simoniacal practices, so that "a great scandal had been engendered among the people." If it could be proved that clergy had secured their benefices illegally, they were to be removed and assigned suitable penance. But even if their offenses could not be proved, the accused clerics were to undergo canonical compurgation to acquit themselves of the charge if there were public rumors against them.[17]

In the case of the Archbishop of Sorrento, accused of simony and other sins, a canon who acted as plaintiff alleged that in cases of this sort "servants are heard against their masters and even criminals are permitted to testify." He pointed out that in the Civil Law accomplices of a defendant accused of lese majesty were permitted to testify, and their evidence actually was given precedence. The exceptions cited by the archbishop against the witnesses who testified against him therefore should be ignored, the canon argued, particularly since public interest required that the sin of simony should not go unpunished because of legal technicalities.

The accused archbishop fought to delay proceedings, alleging that witnesses against him were known to be his enemies; and he supported his contentions by precedents

[16] *Ibid.*, col. 1077. Probably succeeded by Andrew, who resigned 28 May, 1220. Conrad Eubel, *Hierarchia catholica medii aevi*, 3 vols. (Münster, 1898–1910), 2d ed. of Vol. I (Münster, 1913), 137.

[17] Migne (ed.), *P.L.*, CCXIV, cols. 459–60.

debarring such testimony. Nonetheless, his exceptions were overruled, as was his claim that collusion of witnesses against him actually constituted a conspiracy within the legal definition of that term. Frivolous exceptions to the lack of precision in stipulating the dates upon which the archbishop's offenses allegedly occurred were also summarily dealt with by Innocent.

The plaintiff then was permitted to offer his evidence that the prelate had accepted money for appointment to an archdeaconry. Much was also made of the charge that the archbishop had sworn allegiance to Otto IV, with whom the papacy was now engaged in a bitter struggle. He thus had automatically incurred the sentence of excommunication imposed by Innocent on Otto's supporters and had compounded his guilt by celebrating Divine Office while under the ban. The pope committed the whole case on mandate to the Archbishop of Milan, and no further papal intervention was necessitated in view of the offender's subsequent capitulation.[18]

Other interesting papal pronouncements on the question of procedure were issued in connection with the case of an abbot accused of simony and wastage of the resources of his monastery. The case finally was heard in Rome, where witnesses appeared to substantiate the charge of simony. The accused abbot took exception to the characters of some of these witnesses, while the prosecution, in rebuttal, charged that the testimony of infamous persons and criminals was admissable, just as it was in lese majesty cases under the Civil Law. The pope declared that he was naturally as anxious to protect the innocent as he was to ensure the eradication of simony. Nevertheless, in view of the

[18] *Ibid.*, CCXVI, cols. 928–31.

enormity of the sin, "in comparison with which other crimes are as nothing," exceptions to witnesses based upon previous conviction for theft or adultery were overruled. Indeed, even those who admittedly testified because of malice against the accused were to be heard, although with caution.[19]

Not all cases were so serious. For example, the abbot and monks of Premontré appealed to the pope complaining that the Archbishop of Laon had attempted to extort a palfrey from the abbot as the price of his installation. The abbot very properly refused to connive at such an arrangement, which might entail an accusation of simony against him. Besides, all concerned knew that the archdeacon was acting for his bishop in presiding over the consecration ceremonies and had no discretionary authority in the matter. The archdeacon subsequently performed the ceremony in response to categorical orders from his superior, but upon conclusion of the exercises he made off with the palfrey he apparently so ardently coveted. The very naïveté of the offense made it less odious, in Innocent's opinion, than the usual simony cases. But the archdeacon was ordered to restore the palfrey and promise to refrain from such unedifying actions in the future. If there were any delay in making amends to the aggrieved abbot, the pope threatened to excommunicate the offender.[20]

Simony, by the nature of the offense, could easily be coupled with nepotism. The Bishop of Melfi, in one instance, was accused of installing his son as a cantor, although many properly qualified candidates were available. The irregularity of the appointment in question was aggravated by the fact that the cantor "deported himself with levity,

[19] *Ibid.*, cols. 1232–33.   [20] *Ibid.*, CCXIV, col. 174.

so that scandal arose in the streets." It also was charged that the bishop had reserved lucrative benefices for subsequent bestowal upon his grandsons, who were "still crying in their cradles."

Innocent declared that his patience was completely exhausted by the odious sins of the prelate, who, in addition to nepotism, was accused of financial irregularities in the administration of his see for which he had failed to make the amends he had promised before the city authorities. Canons complained that they had been deprived of their prebends by the bishop, who, in some cases, then divided the endowments illegally in order to augment his opportunities for the dispensation of patronage. Clergy of the diocese had been mulcted, with even the death penalty threatened against them if they refused to acquiesce in the imposition of illegal exactions. Marriages were prohibited by the bishop unless the parties paid fees, while adultery was condoned in return for bribes. The pope, convinced that clemency in the hope of repentance by the offender was futile, ordered his deposition and authorized the chapter to elect a new incumbent of the see. They accordingly elected Richerius in 1213.[21]

In 1203 the pope commended his legate, John, cardinal priest of St. Stephen's, for his prompt and decisive action in thwarting flagrant nepotism in Ireland. Upon the death of the Archbishop of Tuam, the legate found the see already occupied by the deceased prelate's grandson before steps could be taken to elect a legitimate successor. The legate, however, "as a discreet and prudent man," expelled the illegal claimant with considerable difficulty and, after

---

[21] Ibid., CCXVI, cols. 625–26. For historical background of division of benefices see Ulrich Stutz, Geschichte der Kirchlichen Benefizialwesens von seinen Anfänge bis auf die Zeit Alexander III (Berlin, 1895), 326–71.

the suffragans were properly assembled, supervised a canonical election. The pope hastened to approve the choice of Felix, Prior of Saballo, and announced his willingness to bestow the pallium.[22]

In 1210 Robert of Poulain, Archbishop of Rouen, complained that abbots, priors, and others who had the right of advowson in his province presented sons and grandsons of powerful personages for appointment even though they were less than twenty years of age or were unsuitable for other reasons. "Clashes and hatreds" frequently arose between bona fide clergy and recipients of such illegal appointments, and many churches remained without pastoral care because of the persistence of these evils. Innocent, "wishing to provide for the difficulties of the Church with paternal solicitude," authorized the archbishop to appoint suitable persons to the benefices in question if those who had the rights of patronage did not exercise them properly after suitable warning.[23]

Grave charges of nepotism in the assignment of benefices arose in the Roman diocese itself, where the abbess and nuns of a convent installed nephews or grandnephews in benefices in an endeavor to "possess God's sanctuaries by inheritance." Mere boys, even idiots, had been installed, and efforts constantly were made to convert properties of the convent into cash for the benefit of incumbents illicitly invested with the temporalities. In some instances a regular plan of succession to the benefices was devised to keep the positions in the family, and tenure by laymen was not unusual. The evil had become so deeply entrenched that when

[22] Leopold Delisle (ed.), "Lettres inédites d'Innocent III," *Bibliotheque de l'école des chartes*, XXXIV (1873), 402.

[23] Guillaume Bessin, *Concilia Rotomagensis Provinciae*, 2 Pts. (Rotomagi, 1717), II, 41.

the abbess attempted to stop the flagrant nepotism, her own temporalities were despoiled and dissensions incited against her. The pope ordered these illicit practices stopped immediately, and no further pontifical action apparently was requisite.[24]

Elections to ecclesiastical positions and promotions necessitated constant vigilance to guard against the infusion of simoniacal practices. In 1212 a canon of the chapter of Bonn complained to the pope of irregularities that had occurred in the election of a provost. One election already had been quashed by the pope, and the canons subsequently were unable to agree upon the choice of another candidate. The pope accordingly referred the matter to a cantor of Treves and several associates, who were charged with responsibility for the supervision of another election.

According to the charge of the complaining canon, a majority then was secured for a candidate "by the intervention of money." The plaintiff offered to make formal accusation and further petitioned that, in view of the corruption already manifested, the chapter should permanently forfeit its electoral rights. Innocent ordered an investigation, directing that written depositions be sent to him if necessary, but ultimately the case was amicably adjusted by local authorities.[25]

Considerations of equity occasionally dictated the exercise of papal clemency for those unwittingly involved in simoniacal transactions. In one case the Abbot of Gemblaux informed the pope that he had been canonically elected and confirmed by the Archbishop of Cologne, since there was a vacancy in the bishopric of Liege in which his abbey was located. But when a bishop subsequently was elected,

[24] Migne (ed.), *P.L.*, CCXIV, col. 1035.   [25] *Ibid.*, CCXVI, col. 568.

he refused to approve the tenure of the abbey by the incumbent, despite the earlier confirmation.

No reason was given by the Bishop of Liege for refusing to sanction the installation of the abbot, who, on his part, as he explained to Innocent, believed that the motive was to extort a monetary payment. The bishop subsequently agreed to the installation, but the abbot then learned to his consternation that some of the brethren of the monastery "who did not have the fear of God before their eyes" had paid money to the bishop to officiate. The abbot professed complete ignorance of these dealings and asked the pontiff if he should relinquish his position because of the simony associated with his installation.

Innocent decided that incumbents of clerical positions who had secured benefices as a result of simoniacal payments by their parents were required to renounce them. The abbot, however, was not related to the monks who had made payments in his behalf not only without his knowledge, but against the general prohibition of simony he had issued. If the abbot had not in any way condoned the illicit transaction, the pope ruled that he was guiltless and should continue to hold office. Those directly implicated in the simony, however, were to be assigned penance.[26]

A rather fine distinction was necessary in response to the problem presented to the pope in 1209 by the Bishop of Clermont. The bishop complained that because of the scarcity of benefices in his diocese he could ordain few clergy, with the result that properly qualified candidates encountered unjustifiable delay in being admitted to orders. Wealthy individuals had offered property to the diocese, but on condition that they or their heirs be invested with

[26] *Ibid.*, CCXIV, cols. 720–21.

the benefices created by the gifts. The bishop accordingly consulted the pope as to the propriety of such an arrangement.

Innocent naturally declared that such a transaction would entail the sin of simony. But if property were granted to the diocese without expressed or implied reservations or conditions, the donor, in response to a subsequent "humble request," might be ordained and assigned a benefice if properly qualified. Everything depended on the presence or absence of a stipulation at the time the property was granted. If the gift were unencumbered by any condition requiring subsequent investment of the donor with a benefice, no guilt of simony would arise.[27]

PLURALISM

Pluralism, or the tenure of more than one benefice by the same incumbent, was another evil against which Innocent contended during his entire pontificate. Legislation and precedent were well established against the practice; Innocent most frequently cited the canons of the Third Lateran Council and the decretals of popes Lucius II and Clement II in ordering the pluralists to surrender their excess benefices.[28]

Early in his pontificate Innocent informed Garnerius, Bishop of Troyes, that clerics, who "animated by the vice of greed," held several offices or benefices when they could be suitably supported by one, were to be reduced to tenure of a single benefice.[29] The pope had learned that the provost and canons of the cathedral of Arles were holding prebends in other churches and often left their cloister, indeed,

[27] *Ibid.*, cols. 169–70. [28] *Ibid.*
[29] *Ibid.*, cols. 170–71.

their diocese, without permission of their prelate. The pope informed the archbishop that he could not overlook a situation where canons regular acted in a manner strictly forbidden even to secular canons. No person could be installed in two churches; but each should remain perpetually in the church where he was ordained so that, according to the Gospel, everyone should persist in the vocation to which he was called.[30]

In the fall of 1198 the pope expressed his extreme displeasure at the conduct of Bishop Conrad of Hildesheim. While serving as bishop of this see, the prelate had accepted election and installation as Bishop of Würzburg, so that "while married to one church he took another spouse in defiance of God." In view of the Biblical injunction, "whom God hath joined let no man put asunder," the pope alone, as the vice-regent of Christ, was authorized to translate a prelate from one see to another. Therefore, when the pontiff, functioning as a delegate of the living God and paying heed to the utility of the Church as a whole, acted in such cases, Innocent explained, it was not man but God who separated the prelate from his original spouse.

If the flagrant defiance of the bishop were left unpunished, others would be impelled to emulate his example. The pope therefore ordered Conrad immediately to surrender all spiritual and temporal interests in Würzburg on pain of excommunication and interdict. The diocesan clergy were ordered to renounce their allegiance to him, and as further punishment for electing the incumbent of Hildesheim as their bishop, the canons were deprived of their electoral right. Since the accused bishop had left his see illegally, he was deposed and ordered not to return on

[30] *Ibid.*, cols. 437–38.

pain of excommunication with bell and candle.[31] His death in December, 1202, ended the case.

Another less serious case of pluralism arose in the archdiocese of Bremen in 1205. In response to a papal mandate, the bishop installed a certain Daniel in possession of a prebend in Bremen, collation to which belonged to the pope. But the chapter refused to approve the appointment, apparently on the ground that there was no vacancy to which Daniel could be appointed. It was pointed out, however, that Herbert, provost of the chapter, had retained his original prebend in addition to the one associated with his provostship. He alleged that it was the custom for the provost to have two prebends and, moreover, claimed that the Archbishop of Bremen had confirmed his possession of both benefices. The pope ordered the Bishop of Hildesheim to compel the provost to surrender one of his benefices in order that Daniel, the papal nominee, might be installed according to the original instructions.[32]

Perhaps the most shocking case in the early part of Innocent's pontificate occurred in the archdiocese of Naples. The son of a former count of Arles, "more by the power of his father than by the free will of the archbishop," obtained possession of more than twenty churches in the city of Naples, as well as a lucrative benefice in the cathedral church itself. "It was not fitting that one should drink to excess while others thirsted," declared the pope, "nor, according to the Sacred Institutes, were ecclesiastical revenues, which were to be divided equitably on the basis of merit, to be assigned to one person while others were de-

---

[31] *Ibid.*, cols. 306–307.

[32] *Ibid.*, CCXV, cols. 626–28. See Potthast (ed.), *Regesta*, I, Nos. 3000, 3299, 3354, 3530.

prived." The pontiff declared that he had noticed in the archdiocese of Naples that when benefices or stipends were to be bestowed, "inexperienced candidates were preferred to masters of arts, the new took precedence over the old, and novices were preferred to veterans who had served for long periods." The archbishop was accordingly ordered to require the offending cleric to surrender the benefices he was illegally holding without appeal. The benefices thus recovered were to be bestowed upon suitable persons who would properly perform the requisite duties.[33]

In the province of Auxerre, too, pluralism had assumed serious proportions. As the pope reminded the archbishop, "dignities and ecclesiastical benefices had been established by the pious devotion of the faithful for assignment so that divine service would be rendered in the Church by their recipients." Yet, "individuals, who did not fear to flout the righteous and pious ordinance of the Church," had usurped many archdeaconries and other dignities for themselves and thereby defrauded the churches concerned of services until public scandal was engendered. The archbishop was ordered to take the initiative in forcing pluralists to divest themselves of their excess benefices if their immediate superiors neglected to act. The offenders were to be permitted to choose which of their several positions they wished to retain, after which the rest would be open to incumbency by other suitable persons.[34]

Innocent inherited several intricate cases involving pluralism from his predecessor, Celestine III. For example, a certain Albert Siccus had been installed as canon of the church of Novara with the approval of the chapter and Pope Celestine. He received his prebend, was assigned a

[33] Migne (ed.), *P.L.*, CCXIV, col. 72. [34] *Ibid.*

stall in the choir, "and by his singing and reading fulfilled all the requirements of his position."

The canon apparently had reason to expect installation in a more lucrative benefice. When one of his colleagues was made Bishop of Calabria, Albert accordingly took possession of the prebend thus vacated without any challenge of his rights. Then, to his dismay, John Torniellus arrived with letters indicating that Celestine had appointed him to the recently vacated prebend at the behest of Emperor Henry VI (1190–1197) and several cardinals.

Albert thereupon sent his brother to litigate in his behalf in Rome. A way out of the difficulty was found, however, when another of the canons of the chapter involved was elected bishop of the diocese. This of course created another vacancy, which Celestine filled by Albert's appointment. But the chapter refused to obey the pope's mandate, alleging that Albert already had a canonry and had received his new appointment by fraud and concealment of the true facts. Celestine apparently had confirmed his appointment to the second position in ignorance of the fact that he already had a prebend. Innocent, upon careful examination of the case, decided that Albert had a valid claim and was not in fact attempting to hold two benefices simultaneously. Unless the chapter could show other reasons to preclude his installation, the pope ordered him admitted at once to the benefice to which Celestine had appointed him.[35]

Occasionally prelates themselves took the initiative in preventing the illegal tenure of more than one benefice by the same individual. For example, Maurice de Blason, Bishop of Poitiers, refused to bestow a benefice on a cleric, who had been presented by an abbess authorized to make

[35] *Ibid.*, cols. 35–37.

such presentation, on the ground that the candidate already had a deaconry, two canonries, and a parish church. The cleric, denied investment with the additional position, then successfully sought a papal mandate to enforce his installation, keeping silent about the other positions he already held. In the meantime, since the abbess did not exercise her right of presentation by naming a suitable candidate within six months after the position first became vacant, the bishop appointed a poor cleric, who, although well qualified, had hitherto been without a benefice.

Judges already had been appointed, however, to hear the case in response to a papal mandate issued in answer to the petition of the original appointee. These judges, in the face of the strong exceptions taken by the bishop, attempted to proceed with the case, with the result that the bishop sent procurators directly to Rome to complain that his prestige in his diocese was gravely prejudiced by the judges, who were animated by personal enmity.

But not all allegations were in behalf of the bishop. The representatives of the cleric he had refused to install because of pluralism claimed that the prelate had gone ahead with the installation of his own nominee while appeal by the original appointee was pending in Rome. In an endeavor to bring about an amicable settlement of the matters at issue, a synod was called by the bishop, only to be frustrated in its deliberations by his intransigency and the violence of his servants. It was alleged that at the height of the altercation into which the synod degenerated the bishop personally knocked down one of the judges.

Innocent in deciding the case declared that the original appointee to the position had no claim on it because of his tenure of other benefices. Yet the bishop's installation of another candidate was invalid, since it was made while an appeal to the papal court was pending. The bishop now was authorized to proceed with a new appointment, with the admonition that he choose an incumbent with the greatest circumspection. In the event the prelate had been guilty of violent disruption of his own synod, his suspension was ordered, but the pope apparently wanted to keep this matter separate from the case immediately at issue.[36]

Prebends occasionally were subdivided in order to augment the opportunities for the dispensation of patronage, despite canonical prohibition of this practice. In July, 1199, the pope addressed the clergy in Euphurdia in regard to an illegal plan which they had put into operation. The revenues of four prebends had been assigned to sixteen persons, with the proviso that the shares of each would be increased as participants in the original division died or surrendered their interests. Eventually, four survivors would each hold a prebend in its entirety. When the illegality of this arrangement was called to the chapter's attention, one incumbent was designated for each of the four prebends, with the succession of the other three to each position promised in prearranged order. This arrangement, too, the pope indignantly nullified.[37]

In another instance, the pope's interests were more immediately involved. He had directed the Bishop of Senlis to bestow a prebend on one Master Henry, since presentment to the benefice in question belonged to the Holy See. The bishop claimed no prebend was available and accordingly gave the papal nominee half the income of a prebend. But the pontiff learned that positions actually were vacant at the time his nominee presented his letters from Rome,

[36] *Ibid.*, CCXVI, cols. 758–64.   [37] *Ibid.*, CCXIV, col. 663.

and these benefices were given to others. The bishop therefore was ordered to make up the deficit in the value of the
prebend he had bestowed on Henry, and the practice of
granting half prebends was strictly forbidden.[38]

On one occasion, however, the pope himself ordered the
division of prebends as a means of curbing absenteeism. The
Bishop of Paris informed the pope that in one of the
churches under his jurisdiction there were twelve prebends.
Since the church in question was located in a rural area, the
canons were reluctant to reside there, and by frequent and
prolonged absences deprived the church of the services to
which it had legitimate claim. The bishop accordingly was
directed to make twenty-two prebends out of eleven of the
twelve. Twelve of these small benefices were to be reserved for the clergy of St. Victor, who apparently had
been serving the church deserted by its own clergy. All
canons who held prebends were ordered to maintain residence in the diocese where they held their benefices.[39]

ABSENTEEISM

Innocent also took strong measures to eliminate the evil
of clerical absenteeism. In May, 1198, he pointed out to
Walter, Archbishop of Rouen, that, since Scripture declares
that "he who does not work shall not eat," it was "unsuitable and unworthy that clerics did not serve the churches
from which they were supported with ample incomes."
The prelate therefore was authorized to take all necessary
steps to ensure the continued residence of his cathedral
clergy in their chapter house so that the church no longer

[38] Migne (ed.), *P.L.*, CCXIV, col. 179.
[39] *Ibid.*, CCXV, cols. 490–91.

would be deprived of services expected from incumbents of cathedral stalls.[40]

Soon thereafter the pope took similar action in the diocese of Angoulême. Here the canons were accustomed to leave the diocese for part of each year to travel about "without reasonable cause." But whenever it was time to assign revenues or to admit new members of the chapter, these absentees hastily returned and attempted to dominate proceedings in opposition to faithful canons who conscientiously discharged the duties of their positions.

Innocent declared that those who regularly performed their duties should receive larger incomes than those who refused to live continually in the diocese. Furthermore, if in the future canons attempted to reopen questions already decided by the chapter solely on the ground that they were absent when the original decision was made, their appeals would be automatically void. As an additional precaution to enforce continued residence, the pope ordered cessation of the practice of installing bailiffs to look after lands and other properties of absentee canons.[41]

Some years later Innocent's intervention was sought in an effort to curb clerical absenteeism that had become a notorious evil in the diocese of Arles. Clergy, especially members of the chapter of the Church of the Blessed Anianne, often were absent, at least intermittently; in some cases they were continuously outside the diocese for a year or more. In an endeavor to enforce canonical discipline, the chapter adopted a rule that no one who failed to discharge his duties for at least half of the year should be permitted to retain his benefice. The time of service was to be computed either as a half year of continuous service or as

[40] *Ibid.*, CCXIV, col. 93.   [41] *Ibid.*, col. 208.

the half-year aggregate of intermittent service. It was further provided that in order to be credited with a day of
service the canon was required to attend Matins and Ves-
pers. The plan, when submitted to the pope for approval,
received his warm commendation and expressions of appreciation for the zeal of the chapter in taking the initiative
in the correction of a flagrant evil.[42]

In the diocese of Ratisbon a different expedient was
utilized to deal with absenteeism. The bishop complained
to the pope that his canons had refused to maintain residence as required by tenure of benefices and suggested that
he be permitted to install vicars to serve in the places of
absent canons. In reply, Innocent declared that "since work
is joined to honors, and the office from which the benefice
arises must be exercised," the absentees were to be warned
once more to comply with ecclesiastical requirements. In
the event of disobedience, they were to be superseded by
vicars paid from the revenues assigned the absentee canons.[43]

Absenteeism by prelates fortunately was quite rare during Innocent's pontificate. In the case of the Bishop of
Ragusa, who was away from his diocese for more than four
years, the pope authorized the chapter to elect a new incumbent within a month after receipt of his letter in order
that the "church might not remain any longer without the
solace of a pastor." [44]

Another serious case arose in the Greek diocese of Gardiki, where, as reported by the Archbishop of Larissa, the
bishop left his charge three days after consecration. Tem-

[42] *Ibid.*, CCXVI, cols. 510–11.
[43] *Ibid.*, CCXV, col. 35. See *ibid.*, col. 1551; CCXVI, col. 815 for additional cases.
[44] *Ibid.*, CCXIV, cols. 970–71.

poralities of the see were left in the charge of the Constable of Romania, apparently with the understanding that the prelate would soon return to reclaim them. He remained absent from his diocese for more than three years, however, during which time diocesan revenues for the most part were collected by the constable. Because of this unusual situation the cathedral church was reduced to such penury that it could scarcely support three clerics. Innocent ordered the immediate return of the bishop to his see, but upon his arrival, the prelate encountered serious difficulty in securing the restitutions of the temporalities he had so unwisely entrusted to lay administration.[45]

[45] *Ibid.*, CCXVI, cols. 299–300.

CHAPTER III

ELECTORAL REFORM

THE MOST immediately significant result of the Gregorian investiture reform was the restoration of the electoral rights of clergy and laity. Yet, within a century electoral rights had become "the exclusive privilege of an ecclesiastical aristocracy—the cathedral chapter."[1] In 1139, Innocent II gave the cathedral chapters the right to exclude monks from elections; this on occasion was interpreted to entail exclusion of the laity as well. Ambiguity on this latter point was removed by Alexander III in 1169 by a categorical exclusion of the laity.

Innocent III held that electoral rights should be reserved to the chapters unless strongly established custom locally admitted others, but in the twenty-fifth canon of the Fourth Lateran Council the laity were debarred, and electoral procedures were defined.[2] Throughout his pontificate Innocent regularly reviewed episcopal elections to assure regularity of procedure and the choice of candidates with proper qualifications.[3] Then, too, since the pontificate of Innocent II direct appointment to benefices by papal provision had been a recognized practice, and Innocent III "was not one to let fall from his hands a right that belonged to

[1] André Desprairies, *L'élection des évêques par les chapitres au xiiie siècle* (Paris, 1922), 7.
[2] *Ibid.*, 9–11.
[3] Felix Rocquain, "Lettres d'Innocent III," *Journal des Savants*, 3d Series, XXXVIII (1873), 516.

him."[4] Nevertheless, the number of direct papal appointments during Innocent III's regime was small, and only in
England was there any complaint that provisions were
granted primarily to Italian clerics.[5]

On a number of occasions during his pontificate Innocent
effectively intervened to ensure strict compliance with laws
and customs governing canonical elections. When diocesan
clergy complained in 1205 that the Bishop of Toulouse had
been elected as a result of the improper solicitation of the
suffragans by the candidate and his friends, the pope annulled the election. But the aspirant continued to hold the
episcopal residence and collected revenues of the see, ag-
gravating his defiance of the papal mandate by appointing
a number of unworthy incumbents of benefices. Innocent
thereupon ordered his legates to assume personal responsibility for the deposition of the usurper and ordered the
chapter to proceed with a new election.

In the case of Parisius, Bishop-elect of Panormo, the
pope ordered the personal appearance of the claimant in
Rome to answer objections to his elevation that had been
filed by some of the diocesan clergy. After the hearing of
the case began, however, Parisius withdrew before the testimony had been submitted, and the pope thereupon ordered
the case terminated by annulment of the election. The chapter was given thirty days in which to elect a suitable incumbent. In the event of their failure to make a choice within
the stipulated time, Cardinal Deacon Gregory was authorized to exercise legatine powers to install a qualified candidate.[6] The pope used a similar procedure in the diocese of

[4] Hermann Baier, *Päpstliche Provisionen für niedere Pfründen bis zum Jahre 1304* (Münster, 1911), 13.
[5] *Ibid.*, 14-17, 29.
[6] Migne (ed.), *P.L.*, CCXV, cols. 683-84; CCXVI, cols. 575-76.

Toul, where, after deposition of Bishop Matthew of Lorraine for perjury and spoliation of church property, two other bishops were authorized to install a new incumbent if the chapter failed to elect a successor immediately after receipt of the papal mandate. Rainald de Chantilly ultimately was elected and served throughout the rest of Innocent's pontificate.[7]

Danger of delay in filling episcopal vacancies was graphically illustrated in the Greek diocese of Nezero. Interim pastoral care of the diocese was committed by the pope to the Bishop of Sidon, who thereupon deprived the cathedral church of its properties and ultimately walled up its gates as a preliminary to converting the building itself into a wine cellar. The dean, cantor, and other members of the chapter were forcibly ejected from their livings and immediately appealed to Rome. The Bishop of Devol then was directed by the pope to compel the offending bishop to restore the chapter to full possession of its properties and emoluments. He further was directed to insist that the chapter immediately elect a new bishop.[8]

Papal decision in disputed episcopal elections often was rendered difficult by the complexity of issues raised or by conflicting testimony as to relevant facts. When the Bishop of Meaux died, the chapter delegated its electoral functions to a committee of three, which was given power to make a final choice and an accompanying promise that the chapter would abide by the decision without cavil. The committee elected an archdeacon known for his learning, prudence, and ability. The chapter approved the choice, and the bishop-elect was confirmed by the archbishop after prior

[7] *Ibid.*, CCXVI, cols. 169–70; Eubel, *Hierarchia*, 502.
[8] Migne (ed.), *P.L.*, CCXVI, col. 897.

ordination as priest and bishop. Allegations that the candidate was below legal age apparently were unfounded in the metropolitan's judgment. The bishop-elect then received his temporalities from King Philip Augustus (1180–1223).

Criticism of the election persisted, at least on the part of some disgruntled members of the chapter. The bishop, therefore, through his procurators at Rome, asked the pope to allay the "jealous strictures." Many testimonials of the new prelate's fitness were submitted at the same time, and Innocent professed himself satisfied on that score. But the disaffected canons also made formal representations to the pontiff. Allegedly, when the chapter originally empowered the committee to act, they did so with the specific understanding that a candidate from the chapter itself would be chosen. This stipulation was disregarded, with the result that bitterness and complaint ensued, with only a few of the canons approving the choice.

In the light of these protests, Innocent committed the matter to the Abbot of St. Victor and the Archdeacon of Paris. According to his instructions everything turned on the powers vested in the committee and the reservations, if any, that had been attached to the exercise of these powers. Further investigation of the newly consecrated bishop's age was initiated, but in view of the earlier inquiry by the archbishop into this phase of the case, the pope believed this issue would be found satisfactorily settled. The opponents of the election subsequently failed to sustain their charges, and the case was terminated.[9]

Papal intervention was not confined to prelacies or to the quashing of elections or appointments already consummated. In 1206, for example, Innocent found it necessary to

[9] *Ibid.,* CCXV, cols. 1366–67.

reprove Renaud, Bishop of Laon, because of his failure to promote a worthy aspirant for clerical advancement. "If you try to promote in the churches committed to you men outstanding in knowledge of letters and conspicuous by the honesty of their morals," the pope declared, "you can earn Divine Grace as well as the praise of men." In view of Master Albert's pre-eminent ability, the pope had directed that he be given a prebend in the church of Laon. The bishop complied with the mandate by investing the candidate with a prebend and assigning him a place in the chapter as well as a stall in the cathedral. Shortly thereafter, however, Albert was "defrauded of his hopes" by the unexplained abrogation of his appointment. No similar position was subsequently given him, although several vacancies had accrued in the meantime. Innocent declared that he refused to countenance this injustice any longer and ordered the prelate immediately to give Albert a position compatible with his accomplishments.[10]

Established custom as well as law was frequently taken into account by Innocent in questions of elevation to, or tenure of, ecclesiastical positions. In one instance, the monks of the monastery of Aumale elected a new abbot, only to encounter the refusal of the Bishop of Terouane to confirm the candidate. The bishop's action apparently was in response to the allegations of the abbot and monks of St. Bertini that custom long had dictated choice of a member of their monastery for the Aumale abbacy.

Both monasteries submitted to the pope appeals supported by a considerable volume of documentary evidence. After personal examination of this evidence the pope decided that it was irrefutably demonstrated that over a

[10] *Ibid.*, cols. 944-45.

period of sixty years seven successive abbots of Aumale had been chosen from the St. Bertini house. In rebuttal, it had been argued that the practice represented a voluntary concession, not a fixed condition. But Innocent held that an established custom had been shown to exist, with the ancillary implication that choice of an abbot could be made outside the membership of the St. Bertini house only in the event no suitable candidate was available. Long survival of the custom of selecting abbots had established a mother-daughter relationship between the houses of St. Bertini and Aumale, the pontiff declared, and a new election in accord with the fixed custom was ordered.[11]

Custom also was invoked in Innocent's decision to quash the election of an abbess of the convent of Newenherse, despite her confirmation by the bishop concerned. After the death of the former abbess, the bishop, who attended the funeral, directed the sisters and the canons of the church to which the convent was affiliated to proceed with the election of a successor to the deceased. Ten of the seventeen sisters and all fourteen of the canons agreed upon a candidate, but the minority of the convent refused to acquiesce in the choice. The bishop prescribed five days of additional consideration in the hope that unanimity might be reached. When the time expired without an agreement, the prelate ordered the case heard at Paderborn.

When the hearing opened, the seven nuns who had refused to consent to the original election presented their own candidate to the bishop for confirmation, to the indignant surprise of the majority in view of the fact that the new candidate was a relative of the bishop. The majority of the nuns thereupon appealed to Rome, taking exception to the

[11] Ibid., CCXVI, cols. 40–43.

bishop's exercise of jurisdiction in the matter because of his relationship with the new candidate.

But the prelate ignored the appeal and installed his relative, although such action was *ipso facto* invalid while an appeal was pending. In addition to the objection cited against the installation, it was pointed out in the ensuing hearing in Rome that the *de facto* incumbent was a member of an ineligible order. Innocent, convinced of the accuracy of these depositions, ordered that the candidate first elected be installed—if necessary, by the application of ecclesiastical censures against the bishop.[12]

LAY INTRUSION

Adherence to prescribed rules in the conduct of elections naturally was impossible if the freedom of the clergy was curtailed by lay power. During the first year of Innocent's pontificate a complaint was received from the Bishop of Aversa in regard to lay influences in appointments and promotions. The pope, in reply, emphasized that he was quick to pay heed to "our brothers and fellow bishops in these things which they reasonably and honestly require." The Sacred Canons were clear in their prohibitions of lay dominance of electoral and appointive procedures in the filling of church offices, and the pope annulled *in toto* all appointments, promotions, and assignments of prebends where lay influences had been invoked in favor of any particular candidate.[13]

The rancors which lay influences might arouse were well illustrated in the case of the election of an abbot of St. Benedict of Bages. The monks properly elected a candidate; but

[12] *Ibid.*, CCXV, cols. 840–43.   [13] *Ibid.*, CCXIV, cols. 55–56.

69

two of the members, "inspired by him whose mission is to disrupt peace," refused to acquiesce in the selection and called upon lay power to support them in their intransigency. A hearing by a papal legate found nothing irregular or improper in the election, which he thereupon confirmed. Nevertheless, the provost of the monastery utilized the difficulty as a pretext to withhold obedience from the newly chosen superior, who had sworn to keep him in his provostship for the sake of the peace of the establishment. The contumacious provost even left the monastery and seized properties belonging to it, so that all the monks were harmed by his actions. When informed of these facts, the pope ordered the deposition of the provost, who henceforth as a simple monk was to be compelled to show obedience and reverence toward the abbot.[14]

A more serious case arose in the diocese of Prague. Upon the death of the incumbent archbishop a certain Daniel was elected, allegedly by improper application of lay pressure, "although neither his morals nor his way of life fitted him for the Church." Innocent hastened to order the Archbishop of Magdeburg to remove the illicit incumbent so that the chapter might proceed with the election of a qualified prelate, and the Duke of Bohemia was ordered to extend all possible aid. The charges against Daniel proved unfounded, however, and his election was finally confirmed in May, 1200.[15]

In Poland, where the pope had ample reason to complain that "the insolence of individuals was rampant, especially in respect to ecclesiastical liberty," lay interference with

[14] *Ibid.*, cols. 24–25.

[15] *Ibid.*, cols. 69–70; see also Potthast (ed.), *Regesta*, I, Nos. 1028, 1211, 1672.

canonical elections was frequent. In January, 1206, all nobles in Poland were warned on pain of anathema to desist from their attempted usurpation of electoral powers in order that canons and other suffragan clergy could hold their elections without restraint.[16]

The pope's interest in the East was constant, in view of his plans for the resumption of the crusade that had halted with the crusaders in possession of Constantinople. In January, 1212, he strongly reproved the King of Cyprus for his efforts to make the Patriarch of Jerusalem interfere with episcopal elections in the church of Nicosia in Cyprus. Not content with the things that were Caesar's, the king was reaching out his hands for the things that were God's, the pope declared. In his endeavor to hold the church in servitude the monarch was dictating the choice of clerical officials, at least by subterfuge, claiming that ecclesiastical custom gave him the right to exercise such interference. Innocent, stating that it was ridiculous to assert that laity should choose the spouses of churches, ordered the king henceforth to permit complete freedom of elections.[17]

Censure of the Count of Tripoli for interference with ecclesiastical elections was coupled with papal admonition to heed the fate of King Uzziah, who had been struck with leprosy because of his attempt to usurp the office of a priest. Likewise, laics who did not hesitate to interfere in the choice of ecclesiastical personnel would incur the stigma of grave sin. When a vacancy in the abbey of St. Paul's of Antioch arose, the count ordered the monks who had the right of election to name three candidates, from whom he

---

[16] Migne (ed.), *P.L.*, CCXV, cols. 1064–65. Citation given by Potthast (ed.), *Regesta*, I, No. 2949, is incorrect.
[17] *Infra*, 175, 180.

made the final selection. The duty of his office compelled him to order such practices to cease at once, the pope maintained, but his action was dictated also by solicitude for the salvation of the count who was jeopardizing it by his actions.[18]

Freedom of episcopal elections was, as is well known, a fundamental cause of the struggle of Innocent with King John of England that began with the celebrated case of Stephen Langton and culminated in the surrender of the kingdom as a fief of the Holy See. John subsequently gave documentary promise to the pope, assuring freedom of elections for both major and minor prelates. In a letter addressed to all English prelates in March, 1215, Innocent announced John's concessions and enclosed a copy of the king's letter. John's submission was another example of God's omnipotence, the pope explained, just as the king's oppression of the prelacy had been a manifestation of Him "who brings it to pass that the tempest blows through the open spaces of His garden as though gently showing man his infirmity and inadequacy." [19]

RESERVATIONS

Innocent found it necessary to act on several occasions to enforce the canons of the Third Lateran Council which forbade the promises of appointment to offices not actually vacant. In February, 1203, the pontiff addressed several abbots in the diocese of Rouen, exercising the power of his office to restrain those who "seeking their own advantage did not fear to weaken the strength of the Church." Complaint had been made that the abbots had promised bene-

[18] Migne (ed.), *P.L.*, CCXVI, col. 747.
[19] *Ibid.*, CCXVII, cols. 246–47.

fices which were not vacant to aspirants who thereupon were granted pensions from the revenues of these positions. This pernicious practice had been carried to such lengths that monasteries were often left inadequately supported because of such diversions of their revenues, and bitter quarrels had arisen among rival claimants for illicit patronage. In response to the complaints the pope quashed all such reservations and grants of pensions. He further authorized the imposition of canonical penalties on any individuals who refused to surrender property or incomes associated with promises of future appointments to benefices.[20]

The monastery of St. Germain de Pré was beset with similar troubles, aggravated by the fact that benefices which were not vacant were promised to candidates "at the behest of certain nobles." In effect, the monastery was paying an annual tribute to certain prospective incumbents of the benefices in question. Innocent, to whom the abbot appealed for relief from the onerous burdens, expressed his appreciation of the devotion to the Roman Church which the monastery had shown for a long time. He therefore was pleased to reaffirm Celestine III's abrogation of the illicit appointments and pensionary grants.[21]

A former abbot of St. Peter's of Le Mans, prior to his deposition, had similarly burdened the house in his charge by promises of appointment and corollary assignments of revenues. In response to the appeal lodged by the new head of the monastery, Innocent declared that "according to the precept of the Apostle, one is required to bear another's burden, and therefore we, who by God's will have received the care of all, are obligated to relieve the burden of those incurring injury as a result of the presumptuous audacity

---

[20] *Ibid.*, CCXV, cols. 256–57.   [21] *Ibid.*, CCXVII, col. 125.

of their pastor." He accordingly annulled the acts of the former abbot which were prejudicial to the monastery's interests.[22]

Equally palpable violations of the Third Lateran legislation occurred in the monastery of St. Bertini, in the diocese of Terouane. Here, too, the promises of appointment and annual pensions to the recipient had been granted only in response to the behests of "nobles and powerful men," seconded, unfortunately, by the endorsement of several prelates. Upon appeal of the abbot and brothers of the house, Innocent quashed all such arrangements with the threat of ecclesiastical censures against those who flouted the papal decree.[23]

Innocent drew a nice legal distinction in his interpretation of the Third Lateran legislation in the case of a clergyman of Terrason. The appellant cleric claimed that his bishop had promised to confer a benefice upon him as soon as possible. This promise was made in writing, according to documentary evidence submitted to the Dean of Soissons, to whom the pope delegated the initial investigation of the case. Yet the bishop refused to make the appointment on the ground that promise of a benefice not actually vacant was illegal.

When the matter was resubmitted to the pope on appeal, he laid down the principle that a promise to appoint to office when the possibility of doing so arose was different from promise of appointment when a vacancy should occur. In many cases, the pontiff declared, "the ability to make an appointment could present itself where the collation was not an expectation of a subsequent vacancy." For ex-

[22] *Ibid.*, CCXV, col. 740.

[23] *Ibid.*, CCXVI, cols. 372–73. For other cases see *ibid.*, cols. 388, 404 (*bis*), 523; CCXIV, col. 55.

ample, availability of new revenues or creation of new benefices could offer opportunity for fulfillment of an earlier
commitment to appoint. In view of the language employed
in the bishop's promise, the Abbot of St. Michael's of Ter-
rascha was ordered by Innocent to bestow a suitable benefice upon the applicant if he wished to evade disciplinary
measures.[24]

The pope's reasoning in the case of a benefice promised
in the diocese of Parma does not appear so clearly in the
correspondence. Gerard of Albani, while acting as papal
legate, informed the Bishop of Parma that collation of the
first vacant benefice was to be reserved for him in his legatine capacity. Later, both orally and by letter, the legate
informed the bishop that the benefice, when it became vacant, was to be assigned to the former's relative, a man of
outstanding learning and morality. The bishop asked a
confirmation of this arrangement from the pope, in view of
the obvious canonical difficulties involved. The pontiff in
reply authorized him to invest the legate's relative with the
benefice. The apparent inconsistency with the law perhaps
can be explained by the fact that the collation of several
benefices in Parma already had been bestowed upon the
pope by the bishop; and Innocent, in confirming the arrangement made by the legate, was therefore exercising his
rights, in all probability after the vacancy had materialized.[25]

PROLONGATION OF VACANCIES

Legislation of the Third Lateran Council dealing with
the manifold problems incident to the tenure of benefices

[24] *Ibid.*, CCXVII, cols. 277–78.   [25] *Ibid.*, CCXVI, cols. 523–24.

had not omitted precautions against the deliberate prolongation of vacancies, whether for the enrichment of interim administrators or other reasons. Innocent was as careful in the enforcement of these provisions of the law as he was unremitting in his efforts to eliminate pluralism and reservations.

In April, 1198, the pope chided Martin Roderici, Bishop of Zamora, for his remissness in bestowing benefices upon qualified and deserving candidates. Scripture taught that "he who serves the altar should live off the altar, and he who is elected to the burdens of priestly office should not be denied the emoluments," the pope set forth. Indeed, the word "cleric" meant "heir," Innocent explained, because clergy, upon ordination, were admitted into the inheritance of the Lord. A subdeacon of the diocese had complained to the pontiff that he was without a benefice, although vacancies existed. The pope accordingly ordered the bishop to support the petitioner from the revenues of the cathedral church until a suitable benefice could be assigned, provided examination by scholars verified the applicant's competence.[26]

Bishops, on the other hand, occasionally sought papal permission to fill vacancies because of the lethargy of subordinates who had the rights of collation or election. In December, 1198, the pope authorized the Bishop of Dunstable to fill offices kept vacant by the inaction of chapters, monasteries, or any other individuals or agencies subject to his authority. In granting the bishop's request, the pope stated that he was following the example of his predecessor who had "excited the sloth of negligent ones to solicitude,

[26] *Ibid.*, CCXIV, col. 68; Eubel, *Hierarchia*, 538.

and circumvented the cupidity of those who wished to apply vacant churches to their own use." [27]

Similar instructions were given to the Archbishop of Magdeburg. The pope declared that he was most anxious to advance the metropolitan in favor and therefore invested him with specific authority to bestow benefices upon qualified persons whenever those who normally exercised the rights of election or collation delayed beyond the prescribed maximum time. Watching over churches and safeguarding ecclesiastical ordinances were special responsibilities of archbishops; the pope as the holder of pontifical power was bound to be a "mirror and example of virtue to others." [28]

Instructions to the Archbishop of Rheims were more precise. In accordance with the provisions of the Third Lateran Council, the pope declared vacant benefices should be conferred on suitable candidates within six months. If a chapter neglected to exercise electoral rights, the bishop, taking counsel with discreet men, should appoint incumbents. In the event he failed to exercise this right of intervention, the archbishop was directed to act. The pope explained that he had written personally to the archbishop rather than relying upon an encyclical, since "more ordinarily is produced from those who receive special concessions than from those who receive only general authorization." [29]

In another instance the pope exercised appointive rights himself when local authorities permitted a vacancy to remain unfilled. In a number of letters to the Bishop of Langres, the pope had directed the prelate to proceed with

[27] Migne (ed.), *P.L.*, CCXIV, col. 433.   [28] *Ibid.*, col. 551.
[29] *Ibid.*, CCXV, col. 571.

the appointments to eight offices which had remained vacant beyond the maximum time. The pope then submitted the name of a candidate of good repute for one of these positions. The candidate was to have the prescribed prebend, notwithstanding the fact that the chapter of Metz claimed the revenues had been dedicated to it for four years. Ecclesiastical censures were to be utilized if necessary to compel compliance with the papal mandate.[30]

Fault was not always on the side of the diocesan clergy. The Prior of Dunstable, for example, complained to the pope that he and the monks of the monastery promptly and conscientiously presented candidates for vacancies only to encounter the hesitancy of Godfried, Archbishop of York, toward installing the appointees. The archbishop allegedly delayed installation ceremonies so that he might continue to receive the income of the benefice. Innocent, holding that this practice "seemed to emanate more from avarice than from respect for the law," authorized the appellants to install their candidates if the primate failed to do so within four months after presentment of a properly qualified applicant. In the period from presentment to installation the monastery was to receive all revenues from the vacant benefice to eliminate any financial advantage to the archbishop in the event he delayed proceedings.[31]

At times, chapters or convents failed to act because of legal complications that precluded immediate exercise of electoral functions. The chapter of Bruges, in one case, had been directed by the pontiff to grant a prebend to a cleric. There presumably was no existent vacancy, and the chapter therefore regarded the directed appointment as incompati-

[30] *Ibid.*, CCXVI, col. 555; Eubel, *Hierarchia*, 293, 307.
[31] Migne (ed.), *P.L.*, CCXIV, col. 1134.

ble with the prohibition of reservations. The provost of the chapter nonetheless intimated to the aspirant that a prebend would be forthcoming, while the chapter expressed its willingness to admit the applicant just as soon as a prebend could be secured. Nothing was done, however, and the death of the provost dashed the hopes of the applicant. He then appealed to Innocent, complaining that the new provost was likely to award the next vacant prebend to another candidate. The pope ordered installation of the appellant and provision of a suitable living.[32]

The issue of possible promises of appointment before the vacancy materialized was involved in a case at Magdeburg also. Two canons of the church appeared before the pope to testify that the Bishop of Praeneste, functioning as a papal legate, had invested one of the canons with a prebend, collation to which belonged to the pope. The chapter refused to install the appointee, and the Bishop of Mersenburg, who had been ordered to perform this function if the chapter were dilatory, was unable to act because he was under sentence of excommunication. The chapter, in extenuation of its apparent disobedience of legatine orders, alleged that the appointment was void, since no vacancy existed when the candidate was presented. After conclusion of the testimony, Innocent decided that the appointee was to receive his benefice if it was vacant at the time he was presented or promised presentation, provided collation of the benefice in question actually belonged to the pope.[33]

Failure to fill existent vacancies was also occasionally attributable to the penury of the church or monastery presumably served by appointees to benefices. In the province

[32] Migne (ed.), *P.L.*, CCXV, cols. 1105–1106.
[33] *Ibid.*, cols. 645–47.

of Bourges, patrons of churches retained such large portions of the incomes that the priests appointed to serve could not be supported by the paltry sums remaining unappropriated. Churches were without pastors, since no one wished to accept benefices that would not yield even the barest living. Innocent, to whom these facts were reported, ordered the archbishop to correct the conditions by whatever means were necessary.[34] It was "contrary to equity and reason that patrons of churches should be filled to surfeit while priests hungered." [35]

In the Hungarian diocese of Zara the cathedral church was reduced to such dire financial straits that a lone canon could scarcely be maintained. "Lest the name of bishop be held in derogation because of the poverty of temporal goods," the pope directed the Archbishop of Thebes to provide adequate revenues for the hard-pressed diocese so that the bishop might care for his flock with true pastoral solicitude and "not be compelled to involve himself in secular business because of the dearth of temporalities." [36]

FORGERY

The pope's efforts to ensure strict compliance with the law in regard to the tenure of benefices occasionally were frustrated by the circulation of spurious letters ostensibly emanating from the Holy See. For example, the archdeacon and canons of Milan received what purported to be a papal letter ordering the bestowal of a canonry on an individual when there actually was no vacancy in the chapter. The chapter therefore doubted the authenticity of the let-

[34] *Ibid.*, CCXVI, col. 606.   [35] *Ibid.*, cols. 745–46.
[36] *Ibid.*, col. 564.

ter and, "as prudent men," sent it to the papal curia for confirmation.

Innocent, in reply to the chapter, declared that the style and script of the letter immediately seemed suspect to him, but for a time his suspicion was allayed by the unquestionable genuineness of the seal. However, closer examination of the seal led to the discovery that the upper part of it was somewhat swollen, and the string by which it was attached to the letter was so loose that it could easily be pulled out of the lead. Evidence of the pouring of fresh lead likewise was found, and the pope was convinced that the seal had been taken from a genuine letter and affixed to one that never could have been issued by his chancery. Any persons involved in the effort to palm off the spurious letter were ordered to come to Rome within twenty days after receipt of the order under pain of automatic suspension in the event of noncompliance. If the guilty persons did not hold benefices they were to be anathematized.

To avoid such difficulties in the future, the pope stipulated that all who sought letters from the papacy should come in person to receive them unless special permission had been granted to send proxies. More scrupulous attention to the format of papal letters was enjoined, and the pope described in considerable detail five types of spurious documents that had been brought to his attention. In the first type a false seal was placed on the letter. In the second type a true seal was affixed to a spurious letter by the insertion of a new string. In the third variant the thread affixed to the seal was cut at the point where the document was folded; false letters then were inserted, and a new piece of thread was fastened under the fold. In a fourth type the upper part of the thread was broken off, and the genuine seal was then affixed to a forged document by a new section of thread fastened to the seal with fresh lead, as in the case of the letter to the chapter of Milan. In a fifth type of forgery, the pope concluded, interpolations were made in genuine letters. Careful attention to the style of the letter and the calligraphy was ordered by the pope, and seals henceforth were to be carefully compared with those of known authenticity.[37]

Circulation of forged letters was indeed a serious matter, as another letter of Innocent, addressed to the Archbishop of Rheims and his suffragans, bears witness. The pontiff pointed out that by the very nature of his office he could not handle all administrative details personally, nor could he defer to the requests of petitioners who sometimes asked him to depart from the ideals of justice and the tenor of the law. But wicked men, undeterred by adverse papal response to their requests, resorted to forgery and thus cast disrepute on the papal office, and also caused other evil consequences of their crime. When culprits were arrested for forgery in Rome, the pope pointed out that he took counsel with his cardinals and decreed that henceforth no one was to receive a papal letter unless he received it in person from the pope himself or an authorized delegate. If an individual had been authorized to receive a papal mandate by proxy he was to send only suitable persons to represent him.

Since the pontiff had learned that spurious letters were being widely circulated in the province of Rheims, the archbishop was ordered to call a provincial council to announce that circulators of false letters would be excom-

[37] *Ibid.*, cols. 1217–19.

municated if laymen, and suspended if clerics. This sentence was to be frequently proclaimed throughout the province and locally in each parish. Persons in possession of spurious letters were to destroy or surrender them within fifteen days, and any suspect letters were to be taken to a bishop, abbot, or archdeacon for examination.[38]

In a letter to the Bishop of Paris the pope declared that he believed it would be proper for a clergyman convicted of forgery to be relaxed to the secular arm after he had been degraded in the presence of the secular authorities who thereafter were to assume jurisdiction. Such relaxation, however, was to be accompanied by a plea that the life of the culprit be spared. If the bishop himself wished to mete out punishment, the pope recommended life imprisonment on bread and water as a suitable penalty.[39]

The Archbishop of Antivari (Dioclea), in Epirus, was reproved by the pope because he had been gulled by a forged letter. Certainly the archbishop should have known, the pope pointed out, that a letter from the Apostolic See used the salutation "brother" in addressing an archbishop or bishop, whereas the appellation "son" was used for a king or secular prince. Furthermore, it should have been a matter of common knowledge that the pope used the singular "vos" in addressing one person, never the plural form. Yet, in the spurious letter the archbishop was addressed as "Faithful Son in Christ," to say nothing of the use of the plural pronoun instead of the proper singular form. In the future the prelate was admonished to pay

[38] *Ibid.*, cols. 1216–17. See also *ibid.*, CCXIV, cols. 485–86; CCXV, cols. 530–31; CCXVI, cols. 755–57.
[39] *Ibid.*, CCXV, cols. 1562–63. See also *ibid.*, CCXVI, col. 794 for parallel case.

closer attention to the form of letters so that he would not again be duped.[40]

Letters concerning the monastery of Burgulens were discovered to be forgeries, however, when suspicion was first aroused by the use of the Gallic term "Burguol" rather than the Latin form. When informed of the forgery and assured of the spuriousness of the document in question, the pope ordered initiation of strenuous efforts to apprehend the person guilty of the forgery and the immediate submission of the letters to Rome for final disposal.[41] In another instance the pope informed the Abbot of Citeaux that letters submitted to him by fugitives from his house presumably conveying papal orders for their reinstatement were forgeries. This fact was apparent, the pope declared, since the purported concessions to the monks did not include the reservation "recipiantur salva ordinis disciplina" which would have been incorporated in a genuine letter.[42]

The papal chancery itself was not beyond remissness, as the pope confessed in an encyclical addressed to all prelates shortly after his elevation. In the press of business subsequent to his consecration, Innocent declared he became "fatigued in both mind and body." He consequently failed to note that the seals attached to many of the letters sent out to announce his election were not stamped on the reverse. He hastened therefore to correct the error by announcing that letters so sealed in the interval between his election and consecration should be nonetheless accepted as genuine.[43]

---

[40] *Ibid.*, CCXVI, cols. 1219–20.   [41] *Ibid.*, CCXV, cols. 1459–60.
[42] *Ibid.*, CCXIV, cols. 1031–32.

[43] *Ibid.*, CCXVI, col. 1221. This incident seems to have initiated the practice of sending out letters of a newly elected pope under a half seal prior to his consecration. P. K. Baumgarten, *Aus Kanzlei und Kammer* (Freiburg, 1907), 164.

IMPEDIMENTS TO ORDINATION

In consideration of cases involving alleged personal disqualifications for clerical office, Innocent's firmness frequently was tempered by considerations of equity that justified relaxation of the law when no impairment of ecclesiastical services was engendered. But when churches in charge of incompetent or disqualified clerics incurred injury, the pope unhesitantly acted to eliminate unsatisfactory personnel.

Innocent strongly expressed his viewpoint in the case of John, Bishop of Brescia. "The olive ought to ripen in the House of the Lord," declared the pontiff, and "the twig planted with access to the waters of growth should return fruit in its own time. If it does not fructify in season it can be appropriately compared with the little fig tree which does not give forth fruit but renders the soil it occupies sterile by its shade." It was perilous for an unqualified person to attain episcopal office; it was "even more perilous for him to retain a bishopric for which his pastoral care did not suffice." A prelate who, conscious of his inadequacy, accepted lower clerical grade descended in the sight of men but rose in inner stature, growing in a lesser position whereas he had shrunk in a more exalted one.

The aged bishop had admitted to the pope that he was laden with grievous physical infirmities, including virtually complete loss of speech. Weakened by debility and illness, he could not even "exercise the power of speech to proclaim their sins to his people—the very people whose blood would be required of him by God." He could not "arise to oppose his breast to the enemy on the day of battle for the House of the Lord, and the Church was deprived of the embraces of its spouse." Pursuing his marital figure, the pope pointed out that "it was more tolerable to be without a spouse than to support the burdens of widowhood while joined to one who was a spouse in name only." In order that the diocese no longer be deprived of pastoral care because of the bishop's inadequacies, Innocent ordered the bishops of Cremona and Vercelli, acting as legates, to call upon the prelate to resign and thus avoid the taint of unseemly ambition. Otherwise his removal, already requested by his subordinates, would be necessitated. The pope instructed his legates to see to it, however, that the bishop be given adequate income to sustain him after his retirement to facilitate his withdrawal. John thereupon resigned and was succeeded by Albert Rezzato.[44]

Innocent rigidly enforced the legislation of the Third Lateran Council precluding clerics of illegitimate birth from attainment of the episcopacy. Almost immediately after his accession the pope was informed by the Bishop of Upsala that a number of Swedish clergy who, "because of the shame of their birth by no presumption ought to seek the summit of clerical orders," nonetheless had not hesitated to aspire to the prelacy. Three such candidates were elected, despite the canonical impediments, but the Archbishop of Lund sharply condemned the elections and refused to participate in the consecrations. Two of the candidates nonetheless were nominally consecrated, only to be immediately suspended by the metropolitan. Innocent approved the archbishop's action and forbade the consecration of episcopal candidates with the impediment of illegitimacy, which, aside from the violation of the law involved,

[44] Migne (ed.), *P.L.*, CCXVI, cols. 656–57; "Decretales Gregorii IX Papae," Lib. VI, Tit. iii, cap. 5, in Friedberg (ed.), *Corpus*, II, col. 939.

would be especially inadvisable "because the people of Sweden are comparatively new in their faith and a great deal of scandal would arise among them in the event of clerical transgression abetted by the hatred of the old enemy." [45]

Minimum-age requirements, too, were affected, particularly when immaturity was coupled with inadequacy of educational attainments for the position in question. Two clerics appealed to the pope from the diocese of Laon concerning disputed disposition of a parish church. Collation to this benefice belonged jointly to the archdeacon and one of the canons of the cathedral church. The archdeacon appointed a youth not yet twenty years of age to the post over the protest of a canon who urged the selection of a certain subdeacon who was known for his learning and morals. Innocent decided that "according to the Sacred Canons, the cure of souls ought not to be entrusted to those below legal age, but individuals who excel in their studies and merits should be preferred in the House of the Lord." The appointment of the youth accordingly was quashed, and the other candidate approved.[46]

When a vacancy occurred in the diocese of Avranches, effort was made to bring about the translation of another bishop to the see. A master of scholars of the diocese appealed to the pope, however, and he ordered the chapter to desist from election or translation procedures without consulting the master who presumably would then report to Rome. For a while the chapter avoided any action in regard to the vacancy, allegedly because of their fear of secular dignitaries. Ultimately, however, they suggested the Seneschal of Normandy for the position, regardless of

---

[45] Migne (ed.), *P.L.*, CCXIV, cols. 420–21.   [46] *Ibid.*, cols. 51–52.

the fact that he was not ordained and was known to be illiterate. Innocent not only ordered withdrawal of this grossly unsuitable candidate from consideration but also directed the canons to account for their disgraceful conduct at Rome. They were strongly cautioned to take no further steps in the choice of an incumbent of the see without the pope's express concurrence in their proceedings.[47]

Instances of the exercise of papal clemency, however, are encountered somewhat more frequently in the archives. A certain Frederick, elected provost of the chapter of Clarholtens, sought papal dispensation to permit his continuance in office notwithstanding the illegitimacy of his birth. Innocent responded that "God established the plenitude of ecclesiastical dignity in the Apostolic See, so that, by diligent examination of various circumstances of persons, places, times, etc., it at one time exercises severity, while at another prefers clemency; on one hand justice is administered, on the other, mercy." Good reports of the competence and conduct of the appellant had been received at Rome, along with endorsements of his appeal by relatives who were known to be devoted to the Apostolic See as well as by Emperor Otto IV, who, at that time, was supported by the pontiff. The pope accordingly issued a bull authorizing the recipient to remain in orders and to be eligible for other ecclesiastical dignities short of the episcopacy.[48]

A master of scholars, on another occasion, sought similar concessions to make possible his ordination as a priest. "Divine Providence, establishing the sacrosanct Roman Church as the head and master of all the faithful," wrote Innocent in reply, "wished the plenitude of power to reside therein

[47] *Ibid.*, cols. 419–20; Eubel, *Hierarchia*, 66.
[48] Migne (ed.), *P.L.*, CCXV, cols. 715–16.

so that it could provide with human intelligence for the punishment or restraint of excesses," but also intended that discretion be exercised in the use of authority. In consideration of the personal merits of the appellant, the pope authorized his ordination, with the caution that he must not aspire to a prelacy without additional dispensation from the Apostolic See.[49]

Dispensation from the impediment of illegitimacy in the case of a candidate for a benefice in the diocese of Cambrai necessitated Innocent's reversal of the decision of the appellant's bishop. The applicant for the position, a subdeacon who had been properly elected and presented for confirmation by the abbot and monks of the monastery, personally appeared before the Roman curia and tearfully declared that he was physically unsuited to manual labor and would soon be impoverished if he engaged in secular business. He freely admitted his illegitimacy, as well as the fact that his father had been a priest.

Innocent declared that the sins of the father were visited upon his progeny as faulty shoots grow from a diseased root. Yet one who by his own merits redeemed himself from the taint of illegitimate birth was worthy of clemency. The appellant was known to be a man of high moral character. The pope therefore authorized his tenure of the benefice in question, but only if there was reason to believe that he would not be "an imitator of paternal incontinence." [50] In a similar case, however, the pope, although declaring that "pure morals are to be preferred to pure birth, and the glory of virtuous deeds takes precedence over the condition and fortunes of birth," limited the dispensation to benefices without cure of souls.[51]

[49] *Ibid.*, CCXVI, col. 875.   [50] *Ibid.*, cols. 889–90.   [51] *Ibid.*, col. 38.

In dealing with the impediment of physical mutilation, Innocent was inclined to be stricter against those who were applicants for orders than those already ordained, although in the latter case the grade of the appellant was an important factor in his decision. When, for example, the Bishop of Mileto reported that his predecessor had installed an abbot who was bereft of his left hand, the pontiff decided that a person "with such enormous defect" could not be admitted to orders. Furthermore, the abbot apparently had attempted to conceal his defect at the time of his promotion, and this was additional reason for ordering his deposition.

A pathetic case in the diocese of Paris involved a priest who, upon the advice of physicians, emasculated himself to prevent the spread of a disease incorrectly diagnosed as leprosy. Sometime after his recovery the priest asked the pope's decision as to his eligibility to continue to officiate at the altar. Innocent responded that if the facts were as represented, the priest should continue to serve, even if his right to do so should be subsequently impugned by others.[52]

Another case of self-mutilation Innocent considered less deserving of clemency. Gerlacus, a canon regular, appeared personally before the pope to seek permission to continue to say Mass, despite a self-inflicted physical impairment. He explained that once when saying Mass "mental negligence" caused him to say the words in improper order. "Since any priest ought to be careful to follow the words of the Mass in the Sacrament of the Body of the Lord according to prescribed form," declared the monk, he tried again. When he again faltered, he was so enraged at himself that he cut off the index finger of his left hand. Innocent or-

[52] *Ibid.*, CCXIV, cols. 15–16.

dered the appellant to abstain from celebrating until he had performed adequate penance, assignment of which was referred to his abbot, who was authorized to lift the suspension upon completion of the expiation.[53]

[53] *Ibid.*, col. 741.

CHAPTER IV

MONASTIC REFORM

THROUGHOUT the history of the Medieval Church, insistence upon strict observance of monastic rules was the usual accompaniment of papal administrative efficiency. Innocent, with unremitting devotion to reform, considered correction of laxity in monasteries a major requisite for the attainment of his broader objectives.

The Cluniac Order, so prominent in the reform movement of the tenth and eleventh centuries, demanded the pope's close attention on several occasions. In February, 1204, the Abbot of Cluny was directed to proceed to the "correction of whatever seemed to need correction" in the houses of the order. He was granted freedom to take any measures he deemed expedient without contradiction or appeal, and any sentences he imposed were assured papal sanction.[1] In further effort to facilitate correction of abuses in Cluniac establishments the pope informed Martin, Archbishop of Toledo, and his suffragans that the Abbot of Cluny was under especial protection and was engaged in the correction of Cluniac houses in Gaul and Spain. The Spanish prelate was ordered to receive the abbot "benignly and obediently in the name of the obedience owed to the pope himself." All possible aid was to be extended to the

[1] Migne (ed.), *P.L.*, CCXV, col. 526.

abbot, whose sentences were to be promptly promulgated and enforced.[2]

The correctional activities of 1204–1205 apparently failed to bring about permanent reformation in the Cluniac Order. In March, 1213, the pope addressed the abbot and priors in a letter of bitter complaint. "If the brethren would only think with diligent meditation," he declared, "they would realize how the monastic life grew up under the Founding Fathers, producing long shoots and the flowers of good works to counteract the deadly poison round about." Cluniac monks had especial reason "to try to be worthy of their tradition—a tradition by which the order, planted in a desert of worldliness, fructified amid many abuses of monastic honesty." The pope expressed profound sorrow that some members of the order were now so degenerate that "they grasped with avid hand against the rule of their order, not denying themselves but filling their coffers." Possessions of the order were being frittered away, so that priories "once flourishing in both spiritual and temporal things were fallen into abject poverty." Immediate measures were ordered to correct the evils, and the pope further directed that reform should be stressed in annual congregations of the order. Loyalty of monks to the abbot, like loyalty of sons to a father, was a prime requisite for the abolition of evils vitiating the strength of the order, the pope maintained, in ordering all members to support reform endeavors.[3]

In 1214 Innocent again attempted to reform Cluniac houses in response to the abbot's complaint that efforts "to

[2] Pierre Symon (ed.), *Bullarium Sacri Ordinis Cluniacensis* (Lyons, 1680), 99–100.

[3] Migne (ed.), *P.L.*, CCXVI, cols. 791–92.

end dissensions, grave scandals, and disorders" were being frustrated by the captious appeals of those who thus hoped to forestall correction of their excesses. Since "the remedy of appeal was established, not for the concealment of evil, but for the protection of innocence," the pope authorized the abbot to proceed with his reforms despite appeals, and the contumacious were warned that they would incur "the indignation of Omnipotent God, as well as that of St. Peter and St. Paul," if they persisted in their recalcitrance.[4]

Innocent did not content himself with directions for the general reform of entire orders but frequently intervened in individual houses where the situation was out of hand. In a letter addressed to John, Archbishop of Gran, in 1198, the pope declared that he was "solicitious as far as he was able for the reformation and improvement of monasteries," in view of his obligation "to plant religion in the churches of God and to nurture the plant." The monastery of Telqui "had fallen into dissolution of order and wasting of temporal goods" largely as a result of the negligence of the prelates immediately concerned. The archbishop therefore was ordered to rehabilitate the house "so that the cult of the Divine Name will be magnified in it from day to day, and the necessities of life for the brethren will be suitably provided."[5]

About the same time, the pope admonished the Archbishop of Arles to exercise greater vigilance over the monastery of Lérins. This establishment, "formerly preëminent in religion and prosperous in worldly goods," now was so degraded that the rule was not observed, and revenues scarcely sufficed for the sustenance of the members. The

---

[4] *Ibid.*, CCXVII, cols. 234–35.   [5] *Ibid.*, CCXIV, cols. 5–6.

archbishop was directed first to try to restore the house to its former condition with the current membership, excluding such individuals as might obstruct reformation. But if necessary, the prelate was authorized to have other monks of the same order transferred to the decrepit house, provided their own abbots interposed no objection to such transfers. As a last resort, the establishment might pass to the control of another order if the archbishop were convinced reform could only be achieved by such drastic action.[6]

Irregularities also were encountered in the monastery of Grandmontré. *Conversi*, entrusted with the conduct of monastery business, rendered no proper accounts of their receipts and expenditures. Furthermore, the ratio of monks to *conversi* had become entirely too small, and *conversi* left the cloister without the escort of a monk and ignored regulations prohibiting absence on the Sabbath. The pope accordingly ordered the choice of two visitors—one a monk, the other a *conversus*—to assume immediate responsibility for the correction of the specified abuses. With characteristic attention to detail the pontiff also directed that no *conversus* leave the monastery precincts with a book of any kind without special permission, doubtless to protect the monastery library against the theft of its treasures.[7]

Irregularities of monks in the diocese of Paris were more serious, since the rule was ignored in matters of dress, diet, and conversation. Innocent was especially disturbed about reports that even the vow of poverty was flouted by the monks, who engendered scandal as well as danger to their own souls by retaining private property. The Bishop of

---

[6] *Ibid.*, cols. 229–30. For another case see *ibid.*, CCXV, col. 722.
[7] *Ibid.*, CCXIV, cols. 948–50.

Paris therefore was ordered to apply appropriate remedial measures. In cases where monks were found living as secular persons, they were to be compelled immediately to enter a house of their order.[8]

In the monastery of Basle, persons who had not taken monastic orders were holding prebends, collation to which belonged to the house. Since the pope "was bound by his office to plant usefully and sow fruitfully for the Lord in the Vineyard of Sabaoth," he declared, "he likewise was required to remove whatever was superfluous by the hoe of discretion and authority." Illegal holders of prebends were to surrender them at once, and the abbot and brethren were ordered to prevent such abuses in the future.[9]

Innocent strongly believed that congregations, synods, and visitations were among the most powerful deterrents to monastic abuses. Shortly after his accession he reprimanded all Premonstratensian abbots and provosts in Saxony for their failure to assemble in annual congregations at Prémontré. The Saxon houses had alleged that they were the recipients of a papal dispensation exempting them from participation in the annual congregations. But Innocent declared that any genuine grant of privileges received from the Holy See would include a provision that no concession should be prejudicial to the order in general. Since absence from congregations was contrary to the rules of the order and derogatory to its best interests, the heads of the houses concerned were ordered to attend the congregations or to ensure their proper representation by proxies. Otherwise, they would be liable to excommunication promulgated by the congregation.[10]

[8] *Ibid.*, CCXV, cols. 1249–50.   [9] *Ibid.*, CCXVII, col. 199.
[10] *Ibid.*, CCXIV, col. 177.

Monasteries in the diocese of Bourges refused to heed summons of their bishops to synods which annually assembled at the cathedral church. The monks alleged exemption from the obligation to attend on the basis of long-standing custom. In response to the bishop's complaint, Innocent announced that any alleged immunities of the monasteries would not exempt them from the obedience they owed according to law and diocesan practice. Attendance at synods therefore was required, and those who persisted in absenting themselves were warned that any reasonable sentence the bishop promulgated against them would be upheld by the Holy See.[11]

In 1210 the pope lashed out against the remissness of French prelates in the exercise of their visitation rights. As a result of their negligence, scarcely any novices were being received in monasteries without the sin of simony. Bishops were commanded to visit all monasteries in their dioceses at least once a year, taking particular pains to extirpate simoniacal practices.[12]

Failure to visit monasteries was by no means always the result of episcopal neglect. Alfonso, Bishop of Orense, complained to the pope in 1198 that the abbot of a monastery in his diocese refused to attend synods to which he was legally summoned and forbade monks under his charge to attend. The bishop then informed the contumacious abbot that he intended to visit the monastery at a stipulated time "in order to recall him to obedience and vanquish evil by goodness." When the prelate arrived, he found the gates

---

[11] *Ibid.*, CCXV, col. 622. See also *ibid.*, CCXVI, col. 312, for an instance in which the pope favored local congregations of noncongregational orders for reform purposes.

[12] Migne (ed.), *P.L.*, CCXVII, col. 198. For discussion of simony, see *supra*, 39–51.

of the monastery closed, and he was unable to meet either the abbot or any of the brethren. The bishop thereupon laid an interdict on the monastery and, when this sentence was ignored, excommunicated the abbot and sought Innocent's confirmation of the sentence.

But the abbot appealed to Rome, alleging that, although his monastery was within the physical limits of the Orense diocese, it never had been subject to the bishop's jurisdiction. Testimony was submitted from some of the monks claiming that the abbot had been gulled into a profession of submission to the bishop some time before the dispute arose. Such submission had been acknowledged without the concurrence of the brothers, however, and with the abbot ignorant of the exemption which the monastery enjoyed. Innocent held that the burden of proof would rest on the abbot. Unless he could produce documentary proof of the immunity of his establishment from episcopal visitation, the bishop's rights were to be enforced, and the sentence he had imposed would be valid until the abbot evinced proper deference.[13]

Obedience was a fundamental monastic vow, and Innocent realized how much his reform program depended upon proper subordination of monks and nuns to their spiritual superiors. In a letter addressed to the Abbot of Prémontré in May, 1198, the pope insisted that "among the desires of [his] heart was [his] endeavor, with God's

---

[13] Migne (ed.), *P.L.*, CCXIV, cols. 52–53. See also *ibid.*, cols. 192–93; CCXVI, col. 582; CCXVII, col. 100. There is no reason to believe that Innocent consistently weakened the bishops' power by partiality to monasteries as maintained by Rocquain (ed.), "Lettres d'Innocent III," *loc. cit.*, 520. Stephen of Tournai's letters reveal that bishops occasionally tried to ensure co-operation of abbots in their dioceses by oaths of obedience. Scheler, *Sitten und Bildung der französischen Geistlichkeit*, 45.

grace, to bring it to pass that within [his] own time religion would better flourish, and monastic rules would improve from day to day." It would be a great blow to the Christian faith if "the rigor of monastic or canonical discipline should be weakened by the carelessness of prelates, or, God forbid, by pontifical negligence."

The pope recently had learned that four canons regular of St. Martin's of Laon had entered into a sworn conspiracy against their abbot, whom they blamed for the economic decline of their house, although actually he had relieved it of a major portion of its debts. When the abbot learned of these intrigues, he chided the guilty monks for their efforts to sow dissension. But instead of humbly accepting the deserved correction, the culprits "added iniquity to iniquity" by assaulting several Premonstratensian abbots before whom they had appeared, apparently, to enlist aid against their own superior. At least two of the offenders, appalled by the magnitude of their sins, then sought forgiveness from the Abbot of Prémontré, but the others embezzled goods of their monastery and took to flight. Innocent authorized the Abbot of Prémontré to proceed at his discretion, with the assurance that there would be no papal intervention to modify his sentences.[14]

Similar difficulties in a Cistercian house necessitated the pope's intervention in 1211. The monastery of St. Jean of Autun had fallen into low estate both spiritually and temporally, and the Bishop of Autun had received a papal mandate directing him to investigate and to apply appropriate remedies. The bishop's efforts succeeded in reconciling the brothers with their abbot, thus allaying friction that apparently had been responsible for the troubles of the

---

[14] Migne (ed.), *P.L.*, CCXIV, col. 176.

house. Then the Archbishop of Langres, on his own initiative, conducted an inquisition into the abbot's conduct. But the pope, in a letter to officials of the Cistercian Order, pointed out that he had received conclusive testimony of the abbot's competence and good conduct. All further proceedings against the abbot accordingly were annulled so that he might continue the reforms already begun under favorable auspices.[15]

Papal action to place a monastery in the province of Besançon under Cluny, because of the notoriously bad conduct of its members, precipitated considerable trouble. The monks rebelled against the authority of the Cluniac prior, thus provoking Innocent to exceptional disciplinary measures. All counts and barons of Besançon were directed to convey properties of the contumacious monastery to the control of Cluny, and secular magnates who refused to comply with the papal mandate were threatened with excommunication and interdict. It is interesting to note that Innocent, so careful to assert the independence of church properties from secular jurisdiction, considered the defiance of the monks sufficiently grave to warrant invocation of secular power to accomplish his purpose.[16]

The most flagrant instance of disobedience to monastic superiors and contempt of vows during Innocent's regime was the conduct of Roncellinus of Marseilles. Although a monk, the offender forsook his habit and usurped control of the city of Marseilles. Here, because of his apostasy, as well as because of perjury, incest, and other crimes, he was excommunicated, and the city was placed under an interdict. These ecclesiastical censures brought the culprit to a change

[15] *Ibid.*, CCXVI, cols. 421–22. See also *ibid.*, cols. 373–74; CCXV, col. 405.
[16] *Ibid.*, CCXIV, col. 103.

of heart, and he resumed his monastic habit, put away the concubine with whom he had lived, and sought absolution for his sins. Innocent lifted the interdict but ordered the offender to come to Rome in person or to send a proxy for his absolution if infirmity or other valid reason made it impossible for him to come.

The penitent thereupon set out for Rome and upon reaching Pisa claimed he could not proceed because of ill health and the danger that beset travel at that time. He sent representatives to the pope, however, and these emissaries pointed out that their employer was the sole surviving male of his family. If he did not control the vassals on his baronial estates, great harm to churches and other religious places would ensue. Moreover, during his sinful career he had committed acts of rapine and had incurred substantial debts; if his properties now were denied him he never could reimburse his creditors or the victims of his depredations. These novel arguments had considerable weight with the Archbishop of Pisa, who accordingly granted absolution to the offender.

But Innocent was not so easily mollified. In a letter of August, 1211, to Raymond, Archbishop of Embrun, the pope ordered that the former temporal possessions of Roncellinus were to be restored to him in the capacity of a temporary executor. After all possessions he illegally held had been renounced, the executor then was to present the monastery of which he was a member with a portion of the property to which he had clear title. The residue was to be used to defray debts of the estate. With the approval of the abbot and the brothers of his monastery, Roncellinus was to administer the property he had conveyed to the house, trying in all things "to be grateful for the favor extended to him by close devotion to his new way of life." [17]

Instances in which troubles in monastic houses were attributable to the disobedience of disaffected brethren could be matched by cases in which the abbots were clearly responsible for the plight of their houses. In 1198 the pope learned from the prior and monks of St. Maxentius of Poitiers that the abbot had flouted his pledges of reform and appropriated revenues for his private use, binding the monks by oath not to oppose these illicit practices. His conduct had impugned the spiritual repute of the house, and all efforts of the community to initiate reforms had been frustrated by the abbot, who had even threatened to invoke secular power against his subordinates. As a culminating outrage, he had bestowed a priory on a layman. Although the accused abbot tried to refute the charges, the pope ordered the Bishop of Poitiers to expel laymen from certain possessions of the monastery. The monks of the house were absolved from oaths they had taken under duress, and the abbot was threatened with ecclesiastical censures if he ventured to resort to secular power to intimidate his subordinates. [18]

Perhaps the most notorious case of misconduct on the part of a monastic official occurred in a monastery in the diocese of Saintes. The canons regular informed the pope that their prior, some years before, had deserted another monastery in order "to return to the ashes of the flesh." He later became a member of their establishment, however, and ultimately was made prior. But his elevation proved

[17] *Ibid.*, CCXVI, cols. 457–58. See also *ibid.*, CCXIV, cols. 128, 545; CCXVI, cols. 52–54.
[18] *Ibid.*, CCXIV, col. 50.

to be the signal for debauch and prodigality, and the resources of the house were dissipated to the point of exhaustion. To meet financial exigencies, the prior created several new canonries in return for payments from the recipients of the appointments. These actions, as well as the prior's chronic inebriety, caused "the honesty of the monastic order to perish where it formerly had flourished." Innocent ordered immediate removal of the offender, who then was sent back to his original house.[19]

Careful exercise of electoral responsibilities in the choice of abbots was a primary requisite for the general improvement in the status of monasticism which Innocent so ardently desired. In addressing the Roman convent of St. Euphemia, in February, 1203, the pontiff declared that "sons, disagreeing after their father's death, do not lighten their mother's grief as they should, but increase it as they strive to tear up their deceased parent's tunic, because, not one in heart, they cannot dwell as brothers in a single household." The monks, "seeking their own advantage rather than that of Christ," had elected an abbot whom the pope knew to be a "religious man, learned and circumspect in spiritual and temporal matters." But the abbot-elect was a member of the Cistercian Order, while the monastery was Benedictine. "The ox and the ass cannot well be yoked together, nor can wool and linen be woven into the same fabric," Innocent declared, in refusing to approve the election. Lest there be delay in filling the vacancy as a result of dissension, the pope promised that he would act like a devoted eldest son providing for a bereaved mother and accordingly announced the appointment of one of his chap-

[19] *Ibid.*, cols. 171–72.

lains as the new abbot. The monks were ordered to receive their new superior as a pastor and father, rendering to him the obedience required by their rule.[20]

The pope was careful also to ban efforts by the monks to couple choice of an abbot with the imposition of conditions subversive to the maintenance of proper discipline. For example, the Abbot of Cluny complained shortly before the close of Innocent's pontificate that when the members of the order considered candidates for the abbacy, they stipulated that they would not obey a new abbot unless he swore to observe the regulations issued by a predecessor. But the newly elected abbot refused to be bound in this fashion, on the ground that such conditions were neither legal nor customary. The pope, supporting the abbot in his stand, absolved him from any commitments he might have been forced to make as a condition for election. The abbot also was authorized to impose penance on the monks who had presumed to circumscribe the electoral functions with unwarranted restrictions.[21]

PAPAL PROTECTION

One of Innocent's most effective measures for the reform of monasteries was the assumption of individual houses under special papal protection. In April, 1198, a monastery in the diocese of Laon was the recipient of such privileges. "It is fitting that the Apostolic See exercise control over these electing the monastic way of life," the pope declared, "lest the incursion of indiscretions of any kind

---

[20] *Ibid.*, CCXV, cols. 264–65.

[21] Symon (ed.), *Bullarium*, 104. See also Migne (ed.), *P.L.*, CCXV, col. 1196; J. B. Mittarelli (ed.), *Annales Camaldulenses ordinis S. Benedicti*, 9 vols. (Venice, 1755–1773), IV, App., 304–305.

divert such persons from their purpose." The pontiff accordingly announced that the monastery was taken under his protection, with confirmation of "any possessions, as well as any other goods which the monastery justly and canonically holds or may acquire in the future by concession of the pontiffs, offerings of the faithful, or other lawful ways with the help of God."

The possessions of the monastery were then fully enumerated, along with a proviso that no one could demand or extort tithes from the house. Clergy, free laics, or properly emancipated serfs who wished to withdraw from the world could be freely received by the monastery, and no monk or oblate could leave without permission of the abbot unless to embrace a stricter monastic rule. No excommunication or interdict could be imposed on the monastery without reasonable cause. If an interdict was in force, the monks were authorized to conduct divine service in a low voice after closing the chapel doors and barring any persons against whom the interdict might be directed. No bells were to be rung in connection with such services.[22]

Even more concessions were embodied in the pope's letter which extended his protection to the monastery of Campo di Santa Maria in Florence. No property could be

---

[22] Migne (ed.), *P.L.*, CCXVII, cols. 11–15. For other examples, see *ibid.*, cols. 132, 150, 189, 431, 509, 1106–1107, 1379–80, 1429–32, 1460–63; CCXVI, cols. 181–83, 275–76, 277–79, 495–96, 566–67, 599–600, 767–70; CCXVII, cols. 69, 103–104, 134–38, 156–59; P. H. Morice, *Mémoires pour servir de preuves à l'histoire ecclésiastique et civile de Bretagne*, 3 vols. (Paris, 1742), I, 732–33; G. A. B. Wolff (ed.), *Chronik des Klosters Pforta*, 2 vols. (Leipzig, 1843), I, 262–63. Many concessions which Wolff thought exceptional are found in charters to other houses. See also Karl Rossel (ed.), *Urkundenbuch der Abtei Eberbach im Rheingau*, 2 vols. (Wiesbaden, 1862–1870), I, 107, 122. In most cases Innocent did not write these letters personally. They were handled as administrative routine by a chancellor and a vice-chancellor. Rocquain (ed.), "Lettres d'Innocent III," *loc. cit.*, 449.

alienated without the consent of the brethren, nor could any pledge or loan be made in the name of the monastery without the consent of the abbot and a majority of the community. Bishops were forbidden to summon members of the house to synods or meetings of any kind. Trials before a bishop or his archdeacon could not be held in the monastery, nor was any secular jurisdiction to be exercised in connection with properties of the monastery. Instead, all civil and criminal cases in which members of the community were involved were declared within the cognizance of the membership, and testimony of witnesses therefrom was to be presumed sufficient for proper adjudication of cases.

In clauses further restricting episcopal rights in respect to the monastery, the diocesan prelate was debarred from interference with the elections of abbots or the removal of an abbot who might be deposed because his elevation had been contrary to the usages of the Cistercian Order. The bishop was expected to consecrate altars, the Chrism, and sacred vessels without charge at the behest of the monastery. If he was remiss in such services, the abbot and brethren were authorized to go to another bishop. A special peace was declared to be in force within the monastery and its immediate environs, so that rapine, theft, incendiarism, or bloodshed within these precincts would automatically subject the perpetrators of such crimes to ecclesiastical censures.[23]

Virtually all papal letters extending protection to monasteries included the provisions enumerated in the case of Campo di Santa Maria. Many additional concessions, however, were granted in individual instances, some of which

[23] Migne (ed.), *P.L.*, CCXVII, cols. 16–19. See also *ibid.*, CCXV, cols. 885–88; CCXVI, cols. 421, 422, 918; CCXVII, cols. 70–74.

further abridged episcopal jurisdiction over monastic houses. The Cistercian monastery of Kappel, in Switzerland, was authorized in the usual way to have its abbots installed by a nondiocesan bishop in the event their own prelate refused or neglected to perform this function. The abbot-elect, however, was also given specific permission to come to Rome for confirmation and installation if he so desired.[24] Such concession also occasionally was enlarged to include direct application to the pope for consecration and blessing of altars, vessels, and vestments, as well as for the reception of monks upon assumption of final vows.[25] The Abbess of Aurillac, in addition to receiving protection against the promulgation of excommunication or interdict by the bishop "without manifest and reasonable cause," was instructed to appeal freely to the Holy See if injured by anyone. Any sentence imposed after her appeal to the Holy See was transmitted to the pope was *ipso facto* null and void.[26] In the case of the nuns of St. Bartholomew of Trebnitz, papal protection of the convent was coupled with assignation of the abbot of a nearby monastery as spiritual guide and counselor of the establishment.[27] In the case of two Cistercian houses, protection against illegal exactions and the abuse of excommunication and interdict was augmented by provisions that any ecclesiastical penalties imposed because of nonpayment of unwarranted charges would be automatically void.[28]

[24] Gerold Meyer von Konau (ed.), *Die Regesten der ehemaligen Cistercienser-Abtei Cappel im Canton Zürich* (Chur, 1850), 1, No. 2.

[25] Migne (ed.), *P.L.*, CCXVII, cols. 173–76.

[26] *Ibid.*, CCXVI, cols. 413–16.

[27] Colmar Grunhagen (ed.), *Regesten zur schlesischen Geschichte bis zum Jahre 1250, Codex diplomaticus Silesia*, 4 vols. in 7 (Breslau, 1868), I, 72.

[28] J. N. Weis (ed.), *Urkunden des Cistercienser Stiftes Heiligenkreuz im Wiener Walde*, in *Fontes rerum Austriaricum*, 91 vols. (Vienna, 1849 ——),

The Premonstratensian Order, by letter addressed to the mother house in 1209, was exempted from the duty of promulgating ecclesiastical sentences imposed on magnates and nobles, even if directed to do so by a papal legate, unless a letter from the pope himself should unequivocally suspend this immunity. This privilege doubtless was granted to minimize the possibility of lay reprisals that might be provoked by participation of the order's houses in the proclamation of general sentences, although Innocent declared that he granted this favor because he "fostered the order with special affection." [29] The Cistercian monastery of Bebenhausen, in addition to protection against illegal tithes, was assured that sentences promulgated against merchants in its service for nonpayment of such charges would be invalid.[30]

Violators of the privileges and immunities of monasteries taken under papal protection invariably were threatened with ecclesiastical censures. In several instances, moreover, ecclesiastical penalties were declared to be automatically coupled with the forfeiture of all dignities, powers, and honors if offenders persisted in injuring the protected establishments after three warnings to desist. Sanctions of this type were intended primarily to deter laymen from the

---

Pt. II (*Diplomataria et acta*, 62 vols.), Vol. I, 41–45. John von Frast (ed.), *Das Stiftungen-Buch des Cistercienser-Klosters Zwetl, ibid.*, Pt. II, Vol. III, 84–85.

[29] Jean LePaige (ed.), *Bibliotheca Praemonstratensis Ordinis*, 2 vols. (Paris, 1633), I, 648.

[30] Eduard von Kausler (ed.), *Urkunden-Buch Wirtembergisches*, 3 vols. (Stuttgart, 1849–1871), II, 346–47. For other cases see Benedetto Tromby (ed.), *Storia critic. cronol. diplomatica del patriarca s. Brunone e del suo ordine Cartusiana*, 10 vols. (Naples, 1733–1779), V, App., 34; Andrew von Meiller (ed.), *Regesta archiepiscoporum Salisburgensium* (Vienna, 1866), 199, 209.

commission of injuries against monastic foundations.[31] In Hungary, where violence against the persons and properties of the clergy was all too common, the whole Cistercian Order was taken under the especial protection of the pope,[32] aside from such arrangements as might be made with individual houses.[33] When necessary, papal protection against aggression was coupled with instructions to local prelates to assure respect for the immunities of the monastery, especially if it recently had been the victim of aggression or spoliation.[34] In Bohemia and Moravia violators of the liberties of monasteries under papal protection were assured their offenses "would engender the indignation of Omnipotent God as well as the wrath of the blessed apostles Peter and Paul," in addition to ecclesiastical penalties.[35]

Special concessions in regard to rights of sepulture also are occasionally encountered in the papal charters to monasteries. A number of monasteries received under papal protection were authorized to provide sepulture if requested in the wills of persons outside their jurisdiction, provided there was no interference with the right of sepulture already exercised by other churches or monasteries.[36] In one case, in the diocese of Lucca, the right of sepulture was joined with the stipulation that if a person within the jurisdiction of the monastery wished to be entombed else-

---

[31] Ernst Hauswirth (ed.), *Urkunden der Benedictiner-Abtei unserer Lieben Frau zu den Schotten in Wien*, in *Fontes rerum Austriaricum*, Pt. II, Vol. XVIII, 17–18; Felice Bussi, *Istoria della citta di Viterbo* (Rome, 1742), 403.

[32] Georges Fejer (ed.), *Codex diplomaticus Hungariae ecclesiasticus ac civilis*, 11 vols. in 47 (Budapest, 1829–1844), II, 341–42.

[33] *Ibid.*, VII, v, 158–62.

[34] See an example in the province of Mainz, C. L. Grotefend (ed.), *Urkunden-Buch des historischen Vereins für Niedersachsen*, 3 vols. (Hanover, 1846–1872), II, 79–80.

[35] Migne (ed.), *P.L.*, CCXVII, col. 149.　　　[36] *Ibid.*, cols. 11–15.

where, his will should include a pious bequest to the monastery concerned, as compensation for relinquishment of its rights of sepulture.[37]

The most extensive concessions of Innocent's pontificate were given to the monastery of St. Paul in Rome. In announcing his protection of the foundation, the pope declared that "when we seem to be conferring anything on you by charter, Most Blessed Paul, surety of our election and preacher of Grace, we do not concede what is ours but only confirm what is yours. By your intercession we receive all that we have from the Father of Light from Whom all good is given and every gift perfected." No one but the pope himself was to exercise any jurisdiction over the favored house, the charter stipulated. The abbot of the house was authorized to celebrate Mass with miter and ring; if ordained by the pope, he could celebrate on the high altar. The abbot furthermore was empowered to ordain to lower orders if he himself was a priest and if such ordination was necessary for the conduct of services within the monastery. Papal permission in advance was declared necessary for pronouncement of any sentence of excommunication or interdict against the monastery.[38]

On occasion Innocent acceded to the requests of monasteries for confirmation of privileges and immunities granted by his predecessor. In 1205 he confirmed the special protection of the Cluniac houses against molestation. In the province of Lyons, Cluniac priors were authorized to excommunicate with candle all malefactors who injured the persons or possessions of the monks if the archbishop or bishops immediately concerned failed to act in response to thrice-repeated appeal. Such censures could be kept in

[37] *Ibid.*, cols. 149–52.   [38] *Ibid.*, CCXV, cols. 91–95.

force until suitable satisfaction was made, and if the gravity of the offense warranted, persons subjected to the ban might be required to go to Rome for absolution.[39] Similar special protection also was granted to the monastery of Camberon, in view of the reluctance or inability of the Archbishop of Rheims effectively to protect the establishment.[40]

Concessions formerly granted sometimes were enlarged by Innocent. In writing to a Cluniac house in the diocese of Amiens, after confirming its rights to receive laics or clergy as prospective monks, the pope authorized it to admit monks of other orders who could not be sustained in their own houses. The house that received this mark of papal favor was declared immune from sentences of excommunication or interdict unless imposed by the pope himself or his legates.[41]

Visitation rights of bishops naturally might engender disputes with monasteries, and Innocent was careful to curb abuses of episcopal prerogatives. In 1198 he wrote to the Abbot of Vladislav, pointing out that the Third Lateran Council had decreed against excessive frequency of visitation. The abbot therefore was authorized to refuse entrance to visitants if the prescribed number of visits was excessive, or the visitation party too large. If a sentence subsequently was imposed on the abbot or his monastery because of his curtailment of visitation privileges it was *ipso facto* void.[42]

Similar issues were involved in the protracted contro-

[39] Symon (ed.), *Bullarium*, 100.

[40] F. A. Reiffenberg and J. J. De Smet (eds.), *Monuments pour servir à l'histoire des provinces de Namur, de Hainaut et de Luxembourg*, 2 vols. (Brussels, 1844, 1869), II, 18–20.

[41] Symon (ed.), *Bullarium*, 99.

[42] Migne (ed.), *P.L.*, CCXIV, col. 124.

versy between the Bishop of Auxerre and the prior of the Cluniac house of St. Germain. The bishop complained that the monastery was recalcitrant in according him his visitation rights, but the prior claimed the bishop was inquiring into matters properly within the purview of the Abbot of Cluny. A charter from Pope Eugenius III was shown which assigned visitation rights exclusively to the abbot. Innocent, in deciding the case, stated that "what belongs to episcopal correction and what to the correction of monastic order" was indeed hard to determine. Violations of the vow of silence, disobedience, and negligence in spiritual things, the pontiff declared, were within the jurisdiction of the abbot as matters pertinent to the enforcement of monastic rule. Yet canonical accusations against a monk would clearly belong to episcopal jurisdiction. Therefore the bishop was to confine his visitation activities to matters covered by the Canon Law as distinct from those comprehended within the monastic rule.[43]

Innocent's connection with the establishment of the famous Mendicant Orders is well known.[44] In more obscure instances, however, he approved new orders and took them under his protection. In the diocese of Tropea, the Florentine Brothers, who lived under the Benedictine Rule, were placed under papal protection. In announcing

[43] *Ibid.*, CCXVII, col. 255.

[44] Of the voluminous literature on the formation of the Mendicant Orders, attention is especially directed to Vladtimil Kybal, *Die Ordnungsregeln des heiligen Franz von Assisi und die ursprüngliche Verfassung des Minoritenordens* (Leipzig and Berlin, 1914), 1–12; Pierre Mandonnet, *Saint Domique, l'idée, l'homme et l'œuvre*, 2 vols. (Paris, 1937), I, 39–51. P. Gratien, *Histoire de la fondation et de l'évolution de l'ordre des Frères Mineurs au xiiie siècle* (Paris, 1928), 6–7, 501. Edouard Jordan, *Le premier siècle franciscain*, in *Saint François d'Assise, son œuvre—son influence* (Paris, 1927), 90–91, shows how emphasis on institutional development departed from ideas of St. Francis.

his favorable decision, the pope pointed out that "neither he who plants nor he who waters the plant is of any consequence except insofar as the Lord gives it growth." The pontiff therefore was bound "to plant the seedlings of sacred religion and water them carefully to propagate their increase, for, if the plants fail to flourish, the new leaves parch, and the stem rooted in the earth fails to grow if the sun and summer heat are lacking." Properties of the new monastery were enumerated and confirmed, and a nominal tax of three pounds of wax per year payable to the church of Tropea was stipulated.[45]

In another instance the Archbishop of Rheims informed the pope of the beginning of a new monastic order in the diocese of Langres. The metropolitan found "nothing that was not religious and honest" in the group, membership in which was limited to twenty brothers under an elected prior. Detailed description of the order informed the pope that the brethren heard Mass each day in addition to chanting the canonical hours. Manual work was required during the day, which was interspersed with twelve meetings for scriptural readings.

The monks abstained from meat and subsisted on bread and water together with one vegetable, from the Feast of the Exaltation of the Holy Cross to Easter. Every sixth day during the summer, and Christmas Day, were marked by complete fasting. Perpetual silence was observed, and the brothers wore hair shirts, although this latter requirement was waived for members who were unable to tolerate its austerity. No one was admitted to the house without a year's probation, and after final admission, no one but the prior

[45] Ferdinand Ughelli, *Italia sacra ex edit. Nicolai Coleti*, 10 vols. (Venice, 1717–1722), IX, 455.

could be absent from the house except for reasons of the utmost importance. In view of the archbishop's favorable report, the pope approved the order and took it under his protection.[46]

ECONOMIC DIFFICULTIES

When monasteries languished because of inadequate financial support, the trouble frequently could be traced to debts illicitly incurred by members of the house in the name of the community. In February, 1198, the pope ordered the Bishop of Ferrara to reform the monastery of Nonantola. The house was in debt, and its poor economic status was matched by spiritual decline; but the abbot's corrective measures fell far short of the requirements. Innocent ordered that if the abbot refused to co-operate with the bishop in effective remedial policies, he would be removed to a monastic cell in Padua. Horses which the abbot owned, in contravention to his vow of poverty, were ordered seized and sold for partial liquidation of the monastery's debts.[47]

The financial affairs of the abbey of Corbeil were involved in considerably greater complexity. Walter, former abbot of the house, had been removed by Innocent's legate, Cardinal Gualo, after the Archbishop of Rheims and the Bishop of Arras had failed to bring about a satisfactory settlement of the monastery's affairs. Walter personally appealed to the pope, however, alleging that the legate's

[46] Migne (ed.), *P.L.*, CCXV, cols. 531–32.

[47] *Ibid.*, CCXIV, cols. 6–7. Although poverty of a monastery and laxity in the observance of its rule often went hand in hand, lay intrusion was more often the cause of the financial difficulties of monasteries. See especially Ursmer Berlière, *Le recrutement dans les monastères Benedictins au xiii⁰ et xiv⁰ siècles* (Brussels, 1924), 6.

drastic action was invalid, and John, chosen as Walter's successor, also appeared at Rome to defend his interests. Innocent learned that the legate's deposition of the abbot had occurred after seventeen months of fruitless investigation and hearings. Action therefore was necessary, or the abbot's derelictions ultimately would go unpunished because of the expiration of the twenty-four-month limitation apparently observed in such cases.

The pope professed conviction that the evidence presented before him established the fact that Walter had involved the house in a debt of £8,000. This sum subsequently was reduced to one fourth that figure, but Walter's mismanagement permitted the obligations of the house again to rise to £6,000. To be sure, Walter alleged that he had spent most of the sum in question in litigation against a Cluniac priory, but rebuttal testimony proved that only £1,000 was thus expended. According to credible witnesses, the deposed abbot had spent most of the money in building a house for himself; according to the monks, the revenues of the monastery, augmented by generous offerings from burgesses of the town, more than sufficed for the support of the establishment. The loans which Walter had made were completely unnecessary, the brethren maintained, and attributable solely to the abbot's avarice and incompetence. Innocent announced that he was satisfied that Walter had outlived his usefulness as an abbot and approved his removal.[48]

Sometimes the pope directly forbade irresponsible contraction of debt. In 1203, for example, he ordered the abbot and monks of Molesme to refrain from borrowing money or making pledges for sums in excess of the maximum fixed

[48] Migne (ed.), *P.L.*, CCXVI, cols. 193–98.

by the regulations of the house. No loan or pledge was to be made except by the consent of the abbot and a majority of the brethren, and then only for the evident utility of the establishment. If any loan subsequently was made in violation of these restrictions, the monastery could not be held accountable for repayment in any manner.[49]

Where creditors were reaping an unjust return from financially embarrassed monasteries, the pope promptly intervened. The monastery of Clusin, in the diocese of St. Jean de Maurienne, was driven by debt to grant the revenues of a certain town to a layman as a fief in return for £80 he paid against the monastery's debts. The monastery had usually received a dish of food each day from the townspeople, together with twelve loaves and fishes on each feast day. Transfer of the town to the layman therefore deprived the hard-pressed monastery of an important asset, while the layman received more each year than the £80 he had advanced in exchange for the fief. Innocent accordingly ordered that if the layman indeed had been reimbursed for his loan to the brethren, the town revenues were to revert to the monastery, whatever the terms of the original agreement.[50]

When expedient, the pope favored temporary or permanent union of impoverished monasteries with more prosperous houses. In 1199 it was pointed out to him that the monastery of Besvens had sustained heavy losses by fire so that it was not able to support the members with even the barest necessities of life. The abbot was thereupon authorized to transfer the brethren to such other Cluniac

---

[49] *Ibid.*, CCXV, col. 769. See also *ibid.*, CCXVI, cols. 402–403, 770; CCXV, cols. 475, 570.
[50] *Ibid.*, CCXV, cols. 868–69.

houses as would receive them. If practicable, the abbot might enlist monks from other monasteries if their skills as artisans or husbandmen might facilitate eventual rehabilitation of the house.[51]

But in the case of a monastery in the diocese of Turin, the pope ordered its permanent merger with another establishment. The twelve monks and the abbot who comprised the surviving personnel of the virtually bankrupt house were directed to place themselves under the Abbot of Clusin. The abbot of this latter house then would appoint a prior to administer the interests of the newly acquired dependency.[52] A similar arrangement was made by the amalgamation of the two convents in the diocese of Paris.[53]

Substitution of canons regular for other monastic orders, or for secular clergy whose administration of their responsibilities had proved satisfactory, was also an important reforming device used by Innocent. In a letter to the Archbishop of Kalocsa, in January, 1198, the pope explained that his office entailed responsibility for the welfare of the whole Church. The monastery of St. Stephen Protomartyr had been successively in the charge of two orders, both of which had plunged the establishment into dissolution. The archbishop, who had been authorized by Celestine III to decide what arrangements should be made for the continued administration of the monastery in question, ultimately recommended installation of Augustinian canons regular. Innocent approved the change and expressed his confidence that it would result in a permanent improvement in the status of the monastery.[54]

Innocent expressed his deep gratification at a change of

---

[51] *Ibid.*, CCXIV, col. 189.   [52] *Ibid.*, CCXVI, cols. 682–83.
[53] *Ibid.*, CCXV, col. 1250.   [54] *Ibid.*, CCXIV, cols. 460–61.

similar character in the archdiocese of Torres, in Sardinia. It was eminently proper, the pope declared, that the archbishop should "wish to eradicate thorns and thistles from the field of the Lord . . . so that the seed, which is the Word of God, would not be smothered, but would fructify fully in proportion to the degree to which the soil had been prudently cultivated." The Holy See rejoiced that the archbishop had committed his vineyard to the care of other husbandmen by removing secular canons from his cathedral church because of their foolish actions and worldliness. If it could be done without arousing undue clamor, the pope directed that canons regular be installed in the vacant places, with suitable provision made for the economic support of dispossessed canons who did not wish to qualify for reinstatement by taking monastic vows. If scandal would arise from so drastic a measure, however, the pope instructed the archbishop to resort to other corrective means.[55]

By authorizing installation of canons regular in the church of Patras, in Greece, the pope also evinced characteristic sensitivity to considerations of equity that were entailed. The archbishop complained that the secular canons were so remiss in the performance of their duties that their replacement by canons regular was urgently required, and he estimated that the revenues of the cathedral church would support sixty incumbents. The pope, expressing pleasure with the prelate's action, declared that not only would an immediate benefit be effected in the church but a salutary example would be set in lands so recently changed to the Latin form of the faith as a result of the Fourth Crusade. Nevertheless, precautions were ordered to ensure dispossessed clergy against injustice. They were to be given

[55] *Ibid.*, CCXV, col. 393.

an opportunity to take monastic vows, and if any did not wish to do so or were ineligible, they would receive suitable provision elsewhere.[56]

Innocent regarded the Cistercian Order as a powerful factor in promoting Latinization of the Eastern Church after 1204. In ordering the reinstatement of Cistercian monks in the monastery of Locedio from which they had been ejected by the Latin emperor, the pope declared that he wished the order could be propagated throughout all Romania. It was an order which "abounding in strength spread itself far and wide, a light not hidden under a bushel but one which diffused clear rays." If Christians in the Eastern Empire would see the Latin clergy embracing the strict Cistercian way of life, their example would cause "the sheep which recently have been again gathered into the fold to glorify their Father Which art in Heaven." The allusion to the sheep gathered in the fold, of course, referred to the prospective union of the Greek Orthodox and Roman Catholic churches which the foundation of the Latin Kingdom of Constantinople had now made possible.[57]

Transfer from other orders to the stricter Cistercian rule was to be permitted, as the pope explained in a letter to the archbishops of Spain. Each should serve where he felt he was called, for the Spirit of God is freedom. While transfer of monastic allegiance was not to be countenanced on frivolous grounds, those who sought such change "with humility and piety, alleging not fictitiously but truthfully that they sought a better way of life," were to be encouraged. If a monk therefore would seek to change to a stricter rule, his superior should acquiesce in the request. Indeed, the

---

[56] *Ibid.*, CCXVI, cols. 336–37, 559–60; CCXIV, col. 114.
[57] *Ibid.*, CCXVI, cols. 594–95.

pope declared, he was ready to grant such requests when they had been refused by the prelates immediately concerned. If it was doubtful that the applicant acted with sincerity, however, the judgment of his superiors would be of great weight "lest an angel of Satan try to disguise himself as an angel of light." [58]

[58] *Ibid.*, CCXV, cols. 1491–92.

CHAPTER V

ENFORCEMENT OF CLERICAL CELIBACY

CELIBACY of the secular clergy in the four highest orders was established by the early Medieval Church largely because the enormous influence of the Fathers had been thrown into the scales in support of the rule. Successive reform impulses strengthened the stand of the Church, and a Lateran Council in 1059 declared that no Christian was to hear Mass said by a priest who flouted the requirement of celibacy. Gregory VII's insistence upon rigorous enforcement of the canons engendered widespread opposition, but the Church refused to modify its stand, and in the pontificate of Callixtus II reiterated the earlier requirements. The Second Lateran Council in 1139 declared that a union contracted by one in the grade of subdeacon or above could not be a marriage. By the time of Innocent III there were no concerted movements in opposition to the requirements of continence comparable with those of the Hildebrandine era. Nonetheless, violations of the canons were sufficiently numerous and serious to constitute a problem, and the scandals engendered by a few instances of misconduct necessitated the pontiff's energetic intervention.[1]

[1] H. C. Lea, *An Historical Sketch of Sacerdotal Celibacy* (2d ed.; Boston, 1884), 71–79, 190–200, 226–40; Joseph Schnitzer, *Die Gesta Romanae Ecclesiae des Kardinals Beno und andere Streitschriften der schismatischen Kardinale wider Gregor VII* (Bamberg, 1892), *passim;* Albert Houtin, *Courte histoire du célibat ecclésiastique* (Paris, 1929), 139–48; E. E. Sperry,

In a letter to Gerard, Bishop of Padua, in 1198, the pope pointed out that "since different orders are constituted in the Church, and more is expected of those to whom greater responsibility is entrusted, it behooves those who are called to the care of the Lord's work to excel the laity in their moral life." The Provost of Feltre had complained that canons, bound to show the right way to the laity by their example, frequently donned lay garb and did not hesitate to cohabit with concubines. Since, "according to Isaiah, those who bear the vessels of the Lord are to cleansed," the pope ordered the bishop to warn the offenders more insistently than he had done. Henceforth he should require canons to eat their meals in the chapter house and to sleep within cloister walls unless evident necessity justified relaxation of the requirements. Failure to comply with clerical responsibilities was to be construed as grounds for immediate deprivation of benefices.[2]

Even more flagrant was the disobedience of clergy in the province of Rossano. According to the pope's letter to Archbishop Paschal, priests within the latter's jurisdiction kept concubines in their homes, and some even contracted de facto marriages. There were instances where priests, after the death of a mate or the termination of an illicit union, did not shrink from contracting another union of a similar nature. The archbishop had tried to call the clergy to a provincial synod, but the transgressors refused to attend, claiming that they were not accustomed to synods on a provincial scale. The metropolitan likewise was defied when he tried to summon the offending clergy to trial and was

---

An Outline of the History of Clerical Celibacy in Western Europe to the Council of Trent (New York, 1905), passim.

[2] Migne (ed.), P.L., CCXIV, col. 269.

refused admission to several monasteries when he attempted to exercise his legal rights of visitation. Resolved to end these scandalous conditions at once, Innocent ordered the archbishop to exercise the powers of suspension and deprivation without appeal, and the absence of further reference to these problems in the papal registers is presumptive evidence of the success of the pope's efforts.[3]

The most shocking violations of the rule of celibacy during Innocent's pontificate were those committed or condoned by Amadeus, Archbishop of Besançon, ultimately deposed primarily for simony, although his other offenses played a part in his dismissal. Three priests of Besançon complained to Innocent about the prelate's conduct. "Ignoring his reputation, he not only failed to avoid living evilly, but making a snare for many souls by horrible and diverse excesses, presumed to sin publicly and shamefully, so that from the candelabrum in which he is fixed to defend his charges he emitted smoke rather than splendid light." The archbishop allegedly permitted regular clergy, even nuns, to marry and return to the world. His own brother he permitted to separate from a legitimate wife in order to contract an illicit union with a nun. Another brother separated from a concubine, whom the archbishop then outrageously installed as an abbess, although she was illiterate as well as otherwise ineligible.

The prelate himself, according to public report, had contracted an incestuous union with an abbess, while a child had been begotten of the offender's union with another nun. Clergy subject to the archbishop's jurisdiction publicly kept concubines, and the archbishop, "defiled by his own graver contagion," did nothing to correct them. Laymen,

[3] *Ibid.*, cols. 822–23.

scandalized by the actions of the prelate, were beguiled into believing that fornication was not a sin because of his evil example. Innocent ordered the Bishop of Gebennes and two other clergy to depose the archbishop unless he could acquit himself with the compurgation of three bishops or abbots, and his removal subsequently was accomplished.[4]

The scandalous case of the Bishop of Vinci was inherited by Innocent from his predecessor. The Archbishop of Ebrun and the Abbot of Bouchaud had been appointed to investigate the charges against the bishop, with authority to suspend him and to send him to Rome for final disposition of his case. The commissioners subsequently reported that they found the prelate "gravely disgraced," but he neither presented himself for a hearing nor refrained from exercise of episcopal functions after his suspension was announced. Celestine then ordered him publicly excommunicated until he personally appeared at Rome. According to reports to the pope from the original commissioners no one was ignorant of the bishop's enormities, which were becoming more outrageous each day. Yet despite the authority of their mandate the commissioners made no effort to proceed further with the case.

The provost and canons of the church of Vinci then complained to Innocent that because of the guilt of the bishop, churches of the diocese were virtually empty, and the celebration of Divine Office was widely neglected. The bishop was publicly consorting with a widow whom he kept in his home, although he earlier had sworn to dismiss her, thus

<hr />

[4] *Ibid.*, CCXVI, cols. 479–81. See J. A. Theiner and August Theiner, *Die Einführung der erzwungenen Ehelosigkeit bei den Christlichen Geistlichen und ihre Folgen*, 3 vols. (Barmen, 1893–1894), II, 249. Eubel, *Hierarchia*, 137, and Gams, *Series*, 555, do not list archbishops prior to Andrew, who died in 1220.

compounding his guilt by perjury. So dissolute was the prelate's conduct that grave damage was incurred, not only in his diocese, but in others, so far had the infamy of his conduct been made known. "Since decayed teeth must be pulled from the jaws of the Church," Innocent ordered the original commissioners to depose the offender and authorized the canons to elect a new incumbent.[5]

Problems of procedure primarily concerned the Bishop of Osma in his campaign against incontinent clergy. He had called alleged offenders before him, only to be confronted by their denial of guilt. No legitimate accusers appeared, and the prelate was at a loss as to how to continue his disciplinary efforts. Innocent, in reply to the questions submitted to him, held that if the offenses of the clergy were of such public knowledge as to be termed "notorious," neither accusers nor witnesses would be necessary to enable the prelate to proceed. But if the offenses were public not by evidence but by rumor alone, the pope decided that testimony by good men as to the existence of such rumor would not suffice for pronouncement of judgment. However, if the suspicion against the offending clergy was so strong that "scandal was aroused among the populace," the bishop was authorized to require the alleged transgressors to undergo canonical purgation, even though no accuser appeared against him. If the defendants refused to undergo such purgation or failed to perform it successfully, they were to be adjudged guilty and punished accordingly.[6]

Somewhat similar issues were involved in the case of the Abbot of St. Stephen of Cornu, in the diocese of Ivrea. The

[5] Migne (ed.), *P.L.*, CCXV, cols. 366–67.

[6] *Ibid.*, CCXIV, col. 605. For efforts to impose additional procedural safeguards see "Decretales Gregorie IX Papae," Lib. II, Tit. iii, cap. 8, in Friedberg (ed.), *Corpus*, II, cols. 255–56.

bishop, accompanied by a priest of Mantua, came to the monastery for customary visitation and correction. The abbot was accused of sins of the flesh and simony, as well as other unspecified offenses. Since no accuser appeared against him, and neither private gossip nor public rumor had aroused notoriety, the abbot took exception to the efforts of the visitors to proceed with the case, and when his exceptions were overruled, appealed to Rome. The visitors nonetheless investigated the charges by questioning the prior and many of the monks of the monastery.

When the abbot's appeal arrived, Innocent appointed the Archbishop of Milan to collaborate with the Bishop of Ivrea and the priest who had initiated the investigation. Since the original visitors had proceeded with the case after the abbot had announced his appeal to Rome, the pope ordered that any testimony to the prejudice of the defendant elicited subsequent to the appeal was to be ignored. The archbishop and his colleagues then reopened the case in accordance with the pope's mandate. When their report was submitted, reinforced by a letter from the Bishop of Ivrea in further explanation of the case, Innocent ordered the deposition of the abbot and authorized the monastery to elect a new head.[7]

Although careful protection of the right of appeal to Rome was characteristic of Innocent's legal administration, he was not slow to curtail appellant rights where they were used to obstruct justice. In a letter to the Bishop of Modena, who had informed him of the adultery and concubinage of some of the diocesan clergy, Innocent declared that "many today, departing from the sanction of the law, assume in defense of their error that relief from its provisions

[7] Migne (ed.), *P.L.*, CCXV, cols. 1505–06.

is to be found in aggravation of their offenses, and, just as they evade the correction of their immediate superiors, they appeal to the Apostolic See without cause." "The remedy of appeal is not to be applied for the diffusion of evil," the pope went on, "but in the cure of excesses." Consequently, the bishop was authorized to proceed to the canonical correction of the offending clergy without appeal if their offenses were "manifest." If the offenders' sins could not be considered "manifest," appellant rights were to be abridged so as to preclude frustration of justice.[8]

The pope on occasion expressed impatience when his decision was sought in cases where the law was clear and explicit. The rectors of the Fraternity of Rome informed the pope that a man who had been a soldier since his youth had married a woman who already had been successively the concubine of two other men. When the woman subsequently died, her bereaved husband was admitted to clerical orders, and question was raised as to the validity of this action. The pontiff, in reply, wrote that surely the brothers must have known such a person was ineligible for Holy Orders. Nothing in the case necessitated papal intervention, Innocent declared, since the law was easy of interpretation, and the facts were clear and uncontroverted.[9]

A question of legal interpretation was submitted to the pope by the Bishop of Ratzeburg. Several clergy of his diocese had been joined successively to two women in *de facto* unions, and the prelate consulted the pope as to the possibility of prosecuting the offending clerics for bigamy. A difficult issue was involved in such cases, Innocent de-

[8] *Ibid.*, CCXIV, col. 546.
[9] *Ibid.*, CCXV, cols. 1463–64; J. H. Böhmer (ed.), *Regesta Imperii*, 5 vols. (Stuttgart, 1870), II, 602.

clared, for "in the contraction of marriage, not the legal effect, but the destiny of souls was to be considered." To be sure, infamy was to be visited upon him who had two wives simultaneously. But those in Holy Orders of the rank of subdeacon and above could not be bound by marriage at all. Therefore "to repute him who has no actual wife a bigamist would be the same thing as the case of a man who contracts with more than one when he cannot enter into a contract at all." Certainly no dispensation from the crime of bigamy could be granted, for members of the clergy could not be bigamists because of the absence of the proper intent requisite for the conclusion of a valid marriage.[10]

The same query was raised by Andreas, Archbishop of Lund. The pope directed him to consider the offenses of clerics in *de facto* unions with two women as cases of fornication, not bigamy. If the offenders sundered such illicit unions and lived continently, the prelate was authorized to absolve them and to permit them to remain in possession of their benefices. In response to another question, Innocent declared that sons of priests were to be admitted only to monastic orders or to orders of canons regular, in accordance with a decretal of Pope Urban II and a canon of the Council of Pavia. The archbishop had also informed Innocent that clergy were living in concubinage, asserting that they had permission from the Roman curia to do so. Innocent naturally condemned these canards and directed the prelate to send to Rome any purported papal letters that embodied such spurious concessions so that effort might be made to determine responsibility for their authorship and circulation.[11]

[10] Migne (ed.), *P.L.*, CCXIV, cols. 605–606.
[11] *Ibid.*, CCXVI, cols. 914–16.

Efforts of the Archbishop of Lund to purge his province of clerical incontinence continued. In January, 1203, Innocent praised him for the strides he had made "in combatting the detestable sin of fornication and indicating the need for clean morals to the clergy." Many offenders "hearkened to his exhortations and rose from the wallow of slime, proposing to be worthy of the Lord in chastity of body and purity of heart." But not all the penitents had persisted in their good resolves; indeed, some canons of cathedral churches publicly maintained concubines for whom they exhibited conjugal affection. The pope, "wishing to apply a remedy for this sickness as far as he was able," ordered the prelate to suspend, degrade, and deprive clergy who failed to yield to his demands to maintain celibacy. In the event suffragan bishops neglected to take action, the archbishop was ordered to initiate proceedings. One difficulty in the enforcement of clerical celibacy in the Lund province apparently had been the refusal of relatives of women in illicit unions with clergy to provide for their support after their dismissal from clerical residences. The pope accordingly directed the archbishop to compel fathers, brothers, or other relatives of such women to receive them and make suitable provision for their support.[12]

Innocent's efforts to enforce clerical celibacy were not always enlisted by the appeals of subordinates. On the contrary, in some instances the pope found it necessary to take the initiative in prodding provincial and diocesan officials into more vigorous action. In 1205, the pontiff chided Peter des Roches, Bishop of Winchester, in whose diocese clerics were known to have publicly kept concubines or committed the sin of adultery. "In correcting the excesses of subordi-

---

[12] *Ibid.*, CCXV, col. 223.

nates," the pope declared, "you ought to exhibit solicitude, lest the blood of those whom you negligently tolerate in sin, when you have the power to restrain them, be required of your hands." The prelate was admonished to force the offending clergy to desist from their sinful practices by prompt invocation of ecclesiastical censures, with especial attention to those whose sins were notorious, although no proof was as yet forthcoming. Otherwise, the pope continued, the bishop would be silent when he should be a preacher and would seem to condone offenses by apathy.[13]

The Bishop of Tournai likewise was informed of the pope's displeasure because of the prevalence of concubinage and adultery among his diocesan clergy. "The shepherd must be diligent in his pastoral care so that there will be no sick sheep in his fold from whom contagion will threaten the whole flock," the pope wrote. If the disease appeared because of the prelate's negligence "he would be judged a hireling by Him whose flock he accepted in custody."[14]

The Hungarian Bishop of Csanád also was directed by the pontiff to take measures against his clergy, who by their sins were "casting disrepute upon the lustre of ecclesiastical purity that should be without stain, and, giving offense to the people, were changing their ministry into shame by their damnable presumption." Some subdeacons and deacons had wives, "if indeed they could be called wives," and while retaining ecclesiastical benefices and dignities were "preoccupied by domestic care." In order that these conditions might be corrected by the industry of the prelate, Innocent authorized him to deprive offending clergy of all income if they refused to maintain continence and make suitable

[13] *Ibid.*, cols. 723–24. [14] *Ibid.*, col. 528.

atonement for the sins they already had committed.[15]

The Archbishop of Gniezno and his suffragans were strongly reproved for granting benefices to men who were known to have concubines, "not even bothering to draw the curtain of concealment over their turpitude." Canons who, "instead of girding their loins and kindling their hands with the glow of good works[,] were conspicuous for their concupiscence and debauchery" ministered at the altar. Sons of priests were allowed to succeed their fathers in the possession of benefices, and on the occasion of solemn feasts some clerics "by their obscene and violent gesticulations" degraded their calling. The pope ordered that all clergy who continued to violate the requirements of celibacy should be ejected from their churches, and the practice of conferring benefices upon offenders or their offspring was to cease.[16]

Difficulties sometimes arose when a married cleric, in one of the orders below that of subdeacon, subsequently became a candidate for a grade that required celibacy. For example, in June, 1199, the chapter of Cambrai elected as bishop a candidate whose promotion from lower clerical orders was legally precluded by virtue of physical deformity. Nonetheless, the election was confirmed by the Archbishop of Rheims. After approval of the election, the Bishop of Arles ordained the candidate acolyte and subdeacon preparatory to admission to the priesthood and ultimately the episcopacy.

[15] Fejer (ed.), *Codex diplomaticus Hungariae*, II, 341.

[16] Migne (ed.), *P.L.*, CCXIV, col. 405. Peter of Corbolio was elected later in 1199 but was translated to Sens in 1200. John of Bethunia then was elected to the Cambrai See, where he served to his death in July, 1217. Eubel, *Hierarchia*, 160.

There was common report, however, that the bishop-elect had married a widow whose son he then attempted to install as his successor in the provostship of Douais. When Innocent was informed of the alleged facts, he declared that if the charges against the bishop-elect were true they could not go unpunished, otherwise "the decorum of ecclesiastical honesty would be confounded." The Bishop of Paris was ordered to investigate and report to the pope. The election was subsequently quashed, and the chapter was ordered to abstain from exercising electoral rights without papal approval in advance.[17]

Another unusual case arose in the diocese of Nyitra, in Hungary. A certain Hugh, while an acolyte, contracted a legitimate marriage. Discord subsequently arose between Hugh and his wife's brother, and the case ultimately was heard before the Bishop of Reus. Hugh refused to be reconciled with his wife, and possibly on grounds of consanguinity, the union was nullified. The woman thereupon married another man, while Hugh was admitted to the order of priest. Some time later, Hugh's conscience troubled him, and with the advice of some monks, he took the Cistercian habit. After his admission to the Cistercian Order, he confessed to his abbot the irregularity of the annulment of his marriage. Apparently upon the advice of the abbot, who admonished him and tried to provide for the salvation of his soul, Hugh urged the woman involved to leave her second spouse, with whom, he declared, she was living in adultery; but she was determined to stay with him. When the case finally was submitted to Innocent for adjudication, he decided that since the woman did not wish to return to Hugh, who had already been ordained, the Bishop of Nyitra

[17] Migne (ed.), *P.L.*, CCXVI, cols. 1265–66.

should content himself with ensuring the separation of the woman from the man with whom she actually was living in adultery.[18]

In 1207 the Bishop of Rochester reported to the pope that a subdeacon of his diocese was ordained to the diaconate without any question as to the candidate's fitness. It subsequently was reported, however, that the candidate was married, and he failed to offer any evidence to the bishop that could be regarded as an effective refutation of the charge. Innocent, in response to the prelate's inquiry, ordered the deacon degraded and deprived of his benefice, with instructions to return to his legitimate wife.[19]

Malice or idle gossip at times was responsible for unfounded charges of clerical incontinence. A woman in Bologna claimed she had been married to a canon of the cathedral, and her case subsequently was heard by the Bishop of Tusculum acting in response to a papal mandate. The charge was not substantiated, however, and the woman thereupon took a vow of continence. Yet, despite the decision, she continued to accuse the canon, who then appealed to the pope for relief from the embarrassment to which he was being subjected. Innocent, after review of the facts brought out in the original hearing, declared the canon had been justly exculpated and ordered that steps be taken to prevent him from future molestation.[20]

Malicious gossip was not always confined to the laity. In May, 1198, Innocent found it necessary to write to the archpriest of St. Andrew's of Pallian in regard to the discreditable actions of a deacon whose scurrilous and mendacious tongue had impugned the reputation of a recently

---

[18] *Ibid.*, CCXV, col. 1179. [19] *Ibid.*, CCXVI, col. 276.
[20] *Ibid.*, CCXIV, col. 126.

married woman of the parish. The deacon "did not blush to allege publicly that he had carnally known the woman," with the result that her husband refused to live with her any longer. "No sane mind is ignorant as to how grave a crime it is for the clergy to glorify themselves when they sin and exult in evil things," declared the pope. The archpriest therefore was ordered to suspend the offending deacon, while the husband was to be required, by ecclesiastical censures if necessary, to take back his wife and treat her with marital affection.[21]

[21] *Ibid.*, CCXVI, cols. 1228–30.

CHAPTER VI

INNOCENT AND EASTERN EUROPE

HUNGARY

INNOCENT especially appreciated the strategic importance of Hungary, Bulgaria, and Poland for crusaders to the Holy Land and as the area wherein Greek Orthodox and Roman cultures vied for pre-eminence. The pontiff was determined to ensure the maximum degree of political stability in these countries in order to promote Latinization of the Church as well as the dedication of their resources to the revival of the crusades. Establishment of the primacy of the leading archiepiscopal see in each of these countries on the basis of unswerving devotion to the Holy See was an important means for the attainment of papal aims.[1]

In Hungary, upon which the pope relied heavily for the fruition of his crusading plans, King Bela III (1173–1196) had been an outstanding example of a capable ruler ever ready to comply with papal mandates, although his kingdom was comparable in wealth with England and France. After Saladin's recapture of Jerusalem the king apparently planned to lead an army to the Holy Land. These plans, perhaps never intended to be taken seriously, did not mate-

---

[1] Edouard Sayous, *Histoire generale des Hongrois*, 2 vols. (Paris, 1900), I, 218. See also Lajos Elekes, *The Hungarian Bastion and the Gates of Europe* (Budapest, 1940), 5.

rialize, but just before his death Bela designated his son Henry as his successor, while Andrew, the younger son, was entrusted with custody of the treasure presumably collected to finance the crusade. Andrew, twenty years of age, bitterly resented his exclusion from the throne, which he passionately coveted.[2]

An implacable enmity between Henry and Andrew therefore arose immediately after their father's death. Andrew utilized the "treasure collected for the pious object" to raise an army and defeated the king toward the end of 1197. The rebel then claimed recognition as Duke of Croatia, Dalmatia, Rama, and Chulmia (Bosnia and Herzegovina). Innocent continued to support Henry, however, and threatened severest ecclesiastical penalties against all persons who aided Andrew against the rightful king. Andrew himself was warned that unless he ceased to incite or condone aggressive measures against his brother, he would incur excommunication and interdict. All Hungarian prelates were notified of the pope's action, and the Archbishop of Gran was made particularly responsible for the enforcement of the papal mandates.[3] Andrew defied the papal admonitions, however, and continued his attacks until he was finally captured and imprisoned after the great battle at Plattensee in the summer of 1199.[4]

Aside from efforts to restrain Andrew, Innocent gave other evidences of his favor toward King Henry. When the king requested that papal pressure be invoked to persuade the Archbishop of Gran to postpone fulfillment of a vow to visit Jerusalem, Innocent hastened to direct the

---

[2] Balint Homan, *Geschichte des Ungarischen Mittelalters*, 2 vols. (Berlin, 1943), II, 4–5.

[3] Migne (ed.), *P.L.*, CCXIV, cols. 6, 227.   [4] *Ibid.*, cols. 227–28.

archbishop to remain in Hungary to provide the king with "indispensable counsel and advice," despite the pontiff's great interest in the recovery of the Holy Land. Since "he, who with reason and the authority of the Apostolic Chair, delays the execution of a vow is not a transgressor," the pope declared, the prelate was temporarily absolved from his obligation.[5]

When some of the prelates of the Hungarian kingdom promulgated sentences of excommunication against Henry's counselors and familiars, the pope decreed that "no prelates could excommunicate any of the king's advisers, absence of whom might prove detrimental to the well-being of his regal person." [6]

Henry's untimely death in 1205 was followed by Andrew's *de facto* accession to the throne. Innocent refused to recognize Andrew, however, addressing him as regent or governor, while referring to Ladislaus, Henry's five-year-old son, as the "boy king." Andrew was admonished to provide his young nephew with solicitous care and education, so that Ladislaus might "find a father in an uncle and a protector in a guardian." At the same time, all the prelates of Hungary were ordered to extend constant fidelity and devotion to the "boy king," to resist any opposition to him, and to defend his honor.[7]

Meanwhile, the pontiff had been urging Andrew to go to the Holy Land in accordance with the obligation presumably imposed upon him by his father's vow. In February, 1198, Andrew was exhorted to carry out "the pious pledge whereby he had promised God to visit the province of Jerusalem with a strong army, but in spiritual meekness

[5] *Ibid.*, CCXV, cols. 14, 15–16, 971.   [6] *Ibid.*, CCXIV, cols. 473–74.
[7] *Ibid.*, CCXV, cols. 595–96, 597, 598.

and humble heart." "Your failure to fulfill this vow will subject you to the bond of anathema," the pontiff went on, "and if you do not depart for the Holy Land your descendants will be deprived of all their rights." [8]

But the struggle between Henry and Andrew alone would have precluded the departure of either, and Innocent, in November, 1203, complained that "petty dissensions have disturbed the peace . . . , and what was pledged has not been realized." Andrew again was ordered to carry out his pledged mission; previous papal indulgence in the duke's dalliance had been "ample evidence of devotion to the king that should have merited his commendation." [9]

The death of Ladislaus, later in 1205, placed Innocent in a new relationship to Andrew, whose title to the throne no longer could be impugned with any prospect of success. Gone from the pope's letters after this turn of affairs are the severity and minatory tone of the earlier communications. When Andrew was merely a duke unsuccessfully contending against the rightful king, or later, acting as regent for Ladislaus, he was vulnerable to papal censures. But with the death of the heir apparent, conciliation and persuasion remained as the only means to ensure Andrew's participation in the crusading project for which Hungarian support seemed so essential. In 1209, addressing Andrew as a "peaceful king of pure heart, good conscience, and unimpaired faith," the pontiff advised that he seek the counsel of the archbishops of Gran and Kalocsa so that, following the example of the First King, Christ, he could "render that which he had promised to God." As Christ had fulfilled His obligation to His Father, so Andrew should carry out Bela's vow. Yet the papal letter included a reservation

[8] *Ibid.*, col. 8.   [9] *Ibid.*, cols. 169–70.

permitting Andrew to remain in Hungary should his absence in the Holy Land jeopardize the integrity and welfare of the kingdom.[10]

Four years later Innocent was still attempting to cajole the evasive king to action. Andrew's request for another three-year delay was granted with the understanding that the "delay was required by him in order that he might send forth more plenteous assistance." "Hence, you, a great king yourself," the pope maintained, "will eagerly prepare to serve an even Greater King and appropriately compensate for your delay by magnificent preparation and provision." [11] It was after these preparations that Andrew finally set out on his crusade in 1216, but Innocent did not live to see even this meager fruit of his efforts in the Hungarian Kingdom.

Papal policies in the kingdom were prosecuted largely through the loyal efforts of John, Archbishop of Gran. Innocent's effectiveness in securing obedience to his mandates was considerably impeded, however, by the perennial wrangling between the archbishoprics of Gran and Kalocsa over the question of the primacy. Gran, the oldest archbishopric in the realm, originally exerted jurisdiction over the ten dioceses of Kalocsa, Veszprem, Pecs, Ipek, Bores, Raab, Erlau, Csanád, Nagy-Varad, and Fehervar. St. Stephen, the apostle of Hungary and the first king to proclaim his loyalty to the Holy See, had been crowned at Gran with a diadem sent by Pope Sylvester II. This fact in itself presumably buttressed the Archbishop of Gran's right to act as the primate of the kingdom. Early in the twelfth century, however, a second province was established under the Archbishop of Kalocsa; [12] and when Bela III was crowned in

---

[10] *Ibid.*, CCXIV, col. 1100.   [11] *Ibid.*, CCXVI, col. 757.
[12] Homan, *Geschichte des Ungarischen Mittelalters*, II, 5.

1173 by this same archbishop, serious doubts arose as to which of the provinces enjoyed pre-eminence.

Innocent, in a letter to the Archbishop of Gran, explicitly reaffirmed the primacy of the older province. "The matter of Bela's acceptance of the crown from the church at Kalocsa," he declared, "does not overrule what has been recorded by our blessed predecessor (Pope Clement III), namely that all Hungarian kings should be crowned by the Archbishop of Gran, whose status as metropolitan has been manifestly recognized." An enumeration of the other rights appertaining solely to the church of Gran followed: "In the matter of bestowing ecclesiastical sacraments upon the kings and queens of Hungary and their successors and in all questions necessitating church jurisdiction—royal and official provostships, the collection of tithes, and the supervision of abbeys—all Hungary is subject to the church of Gran. Accordingly, the authority of the Apostolic Chair confirms that knowledge of all church laws and customs pertains to you and your successors." [13] Shortly thereafter, Innocent, again confirming the right of the church of Gran to rule on all issues involving abbeys and royal provostships, warned the primate to guard against "impostors and those who might prejudice either him or his successors in such matters." [14]

The pope's unqualified defense of the primacy of Gran apparently did not result in a *rapprochement* between the two archbishoprics, for, in 1209, Innocent once more adverted to the subject of Bela III's coronation. Addressing himself to the Archbishop of Gran, the pope contended that sheer necessity had warranted Bella's coronation by the Archbishop of Kalocsa, but this act in no wise was in-

[13] Migne (ed.), *P.L.*, CCXV, col. 56. [14] *Ibid.*

tended to prejudice the traditional privileges of the province of Gran. The pontiff quoted Bela's own words in corroboration of this point: "I, Bela, King of Hungary, Dalmatia, Croatia, and Rama, by the grace of God disposed to divine mercy, take the crown from the Archbishop of Kalocsa, but not in prejudice of the church at Gran inasmuch as Hungarian kings should always be crowned by its archbishop." [15] The pope also availed himself of an opportunity to indicate that all things, particularly salvation, derived from the authority of the Apostolic Chair. "No man," Innocent decreed, "unless he be deemed unworthy of the Omnipotent God and his blessed Apostles, Peter and Paul, will be allowed either to infringe upon our confirmation or temerariously to contradict it." [16] An epitomized version of this same letter subsequently was sent to all other prelates attached to the church of Gran.[17]

The year 1211–1212 witnessed another eruption of differences between the rival provinces. Innocent called upon Andrew, whom he had recognized as king after the death of Ladislaus, to facilitate a reconciliation between the archbishops and clergy of lower rank of both churches. The pontiff cautioned Andrew to effect an agreement "without prejudice to either church and in a manner both amicable and in accordance with God's will." Settlement of the grievances was to be the exclusive prerogative of the Apostolic Chair, and Innocent painstakingly stressed that the king should in no way impugn the absolute jurisdiction of the Church over all questions of an ecclesiastical nature.[18]

In February, 1212, Innocent apprised Andrew of the conclusion of peace between the archbishops of Gran and

---

[15] *Ibid.*, CCXVI, cols. 50–51.   [16] *Ibid.*
[17] *Ibid.*, cols. 51–52.   [18] *Ibid.*, cols. 447–48.

Kalocsa.[19] While the rights of coronation and coinage were assigned definitely to the church of Gran, certain noteworthy concessions were made to the younger province. The Archbishop of Gran renounced all his former jurisdictional prerogatives in the province of Kalocsa, and the privilege of conferring the sacraments upon members of the royal family, previously reserved to the church of Gran, could now be exercised by either church, contingent upon the king's option in the matter.[20]

No unusual condition or adverse circumstances, the pope ruled, could nullify or impair the right of the archbishops of Gran to crown all future Hungarian kings. The pope maintained that "the first crowning of the Hungarian king is especially regarded as the sole right of the Church at Gran; and even if the Archbishop of Gran is unable, or knavishly refuses, to crown the king, or if he vacates the church, and the king therefore is crowned at Kalocsa, nothing in such a coronation can engender a claim to the initial right of coronation." In other respects the two churches promised to conserve and safeguard their ancient customs and liberties. They further pledged themselves to constant compliance with all of the provisions of the reconciliation the pope had fostered. Innocent reiterated that all infringements upon the terms of the agreement would be offenses against the Holy See, the sole and supreme fount of all authority and salvation.[21]

The conversion of pagans and the return of schismatics to the Roman Church were also matters with which Innocent was constantly concerned, in line with his conception

---

[19] *Ibid.*, col. 515.　　　　　　　　[20] *Ibid.*, col. 516.
[21] *Ibid.*, col. 515.

of an ecclesiastical commonwealth consisting of all nations under the spiritual control and temporal tutelage of the pope. Serbia, a vassal state of the Magyar kingdom, was especially susceptible to inducements from the Holy See, inasmuch as it, like Bulgaria, had been subjugated by the Byzantine Empire.

In December, 1202, Innocent commended King Henry of Hungary for his work in aiding the unification and Latinization of the churches in Serbia. After an encomium on Hungary's fealty and devotion to the Holy See, the pope wrote: "Inasmuch as you have evinced constant and regal solicitude regarding the land of the zhupan, you will be pleased by the news that we are sending a legate to Serbia. We are eager to inform you of this fact and urge that you defer in all ways to the legate's suggestions." The pontiff also apostrophized Henry in regard to his subservience to papal decrees: "We advise your supernal majesty to serve, first of all, the institutions of the Roman Church . . . and to reduce yourself completely to obedience, so that you and your kingdom will become faithful members of the one flock under the one shepherd." [22]

Innocent subsequently admonished the zhupan to return to the Catholic faith, and to manifest, in the presence of the Archbishop of Kalocsa, his willingness to revere and obey the pope. The pontiff declared that the Serbian ruler should "aspire efficaciously" toward papal honor and protection,[23] for such aspiration, Innocent believed, was consonant with the will of God. The pope declared that "the God-Man, Jesus Christ, judge of all men, established the primacy of the Apostolic Chair in the person of the Apostle,

[22] *Ibid.*, CCXIV, col. 971.   [23] *Ibid.*

the Blessed Peter, to whom, before His Passion, He addressed Himself in the words 'thou art Peter, and on this rock I will build my church.' " [24]

The Archbishop of Kalocsa likewise received instructions from the Holy See revelant to the conversion of the zhupan and other Serbian prelates formerly "steeped in the Orthodox Faith" and spiritually subservient to the Patriarch of Constantinople. All such Serbian prelates and nobles were commanded to take oaths of obedience and good faith in the presence of the archbishop, and to denounce, "eternally and absolutely," the authority of the patriarch. The condemnation of the Orthodox metropolitan contrasted sharply with the attitude which the converts were expected to assume toward the Archbishop of Kalocsa and his suffragans. "Receive from them," Innocent directed, "respect and reverence for our physical persons, as these support and attest to our authority." [25]

Equal in importance to the replacement of the Greek faith by Roman Catholicism was the extirpation of heresy, particularly Catharism. In 1200 the pope enunciated certain punishments and proscriptions to be imposed upon Cathari loyal to the nobleman, Culini Bani. Those who favored or befriended the "infamous ones" were likewise to be proscribed. Bishops and archbishops, Innocent ordered, were to be excluded from all districts that favored, received, or defended heretics. Apostates were forbidden to occupy public offices and denied the rights of sanctuary and testimony within cities. Heretical priests were divested of all benefices and privileges; and all persons who failed to avoid them incurred sentences of anathema. A recalcitrant bishop, Nicholas of Fehervar, was anathematized, and King

[24] *Ibid.*   [25] *Ibid.*, CCXV, col. 29.

Henry was invested with the responsibility of compelling the transgressor to recant.[26]

Bernard, Bishop of Veszprem, was instructed similarly to expel Bani and his followers from all parts of his diocese. All heretics were to be denounced publicly, and their possessions were to be confiscated. Only those in their midst who still professed themselves Catholics were to be spared banishment, but they nonetheless were to come to Rome "there to make professions of their faith and sincerity before the Apostolic Chair, alone capable of confirming the good and rejecting the bad." [27]

BULGARIA

The history of Innocent's relations with Bulgaria was bound inextricably with that state's determination to achieve permanent independence from the Byzantine Empire. In the latter half of the twelfth century two brothers of royal lineage, the boyars Asa and Peter, were emboldened by the chaotic condition of the empire to demand equal rights for their Bulgarian subjects. The emperor ignored their complaints, with the result that a revolt ensued, and in 1186 Asa I became tsar after defeating a Byzantine army at Stara Planina. The new tsar was assassinated with Byzantine connivance in 1190, however, and was succeeded by Peter, who shortly thereafter shared his brother's fate.

A third brother, Johannitsa, then acceded to the throne. He had spent considerable time at the Byzantine court as a hostage and had conceived an implacable hatred for the Byzantines, while mastering the details of their ad-

[26] *Ibid.*, CCXIV, cols. 871–72.
[27] *Ibid.*, col. 1108. C. A. Ferrario, *Storia dei Bulgari* (Milan, 1940), 73–74; Wilhelm Ruland, *Geschichte der Bulgaren* (Berlin, 1911), 38.

ministrative system. After an agreement with Alexius III, Johannitsa, by shrewd and unscrupulous measures, extended the confines of Bulgaria and converted it into one of the most powerful states of eastern Europe. At its zenith the empire, comprising the conquered principalities of Nis, Belgrade, Branitchevo, Prizrend, Uskub, and Kustundil, extended from Thessaly to Sofia.

Intent upon the protection of his empire's independence, Johannitsa sought to remove the Bulgar Church from the influence of the Patriarch of Constantinople. Above all, he desired a patriarch whose see would be in Bulgaria and who would be vested with authority to anoint and crown the ruler of the kingdom. Johannitsa naturally looked to the pope for the accomplishment of his ends, and as early as 1197 he wrote to Rome relevant to his coronation. For inexplicable reasons this initial overture by Johannitsa elicited no response from the Holy See.[28] But in 1199 Innocent sent as an envoy Dominic, Greek Archpresbyter of Brindisi, to Johannitsa's court.[29] Dominic remained in Bulgaria until 1202, when he returned to Rome with the tsar's representative, Blaise, Bishop of Branitchevo, who carried a personal letter from Johannitsa to the Holy Father.[30]

Johannitsa's letter was both unctuous and ingratiating. He deemed Innocent's letters "more valuable than all the gold and precious stones in the world," and he humbly expressed a desire to emulate his predecessors by joining the

[28] Constantin Jireček, *Geschichte der Serben,* 2 vols. (Gotha, 1911), I, 283; R. P. Guérin-Songéon, *Histoire de la Bulgarie depuis les origines jusqu'à nos jours* (Paris, 1913), 238, 239, 240, 285; Minco Scipovensky, *La Bulgaria, XVI secoli di storia e Boris III zar dei Bulgari* (Milan, 1931), 55.

[29] Migne (ed.), *P.L.,* CCXIV, col. 825.

[30] Guérin-Songéon, *Bulgarie,* 240.

Roman Church, "Our Mother, the crown and recognition of our dignity." [31]

In his reply to the tsar, Innocent delineated the futility of past attempts to establish a lasting relationship between Bulgaria and the Apostolic Chair. Preceding popes, especially Nicholas I, had sent legates to Bulgaria, only to have the Greeks thwart their efforts to bring the nation into the Roman fold. Nevertheless, Innocent apprized Johannitsa of his intention to send a legate, John of Casemarino, to Bulgaria so that abuses and evils there "might be set right and rectified in accordance with the will of God." [32] Prince Bellota and other nobles simultaneously were admonished to accord the legate a "benevolent reception" and to persevere in their fealty to the Church. [33]

Upon learning of the negotiations in progress between the pope and Johannitsa, the Byzantines offered the latter the title of tsar and the imperial crown, [34] but he hastened to inform Innocent of his rejection of the offer. "I wish to be the servant of Saint Peter and Your Holiness," the tsar declared; "I beseech you, then, to send a cardinal to crown me and to establish a patriarchate in my realm." The tsar explicitly recognized Innocent as the successor of Peter, to whom God had bequeathed the power "to bind and loose" all men on earth. [35]

In July, 1203, Archbishop Basil of Tirnova, carrying Johannitsa's letter, left Bulgaria for Durazzo, where he was hospitably received by a Count Walter. [36] The Byzantines, however, subsequently imprisoned the prelate, threatening to throw him into the sea unless he abandoned his

---

[31] Migne (ed.), *P.L.*, CCXIV, cols. 1112–13.   [32] *Ibid.*, cols. 1113–15.
[33] *Ibid.*, col. 1118.   [34] Guérin-Songéon, *Bulgarie*, 241.
[35] Migne (ed.), *P.L.*, CCXV, cols. 155–56.
[36] Guérin-Songéon, *Bulgarie*, 241.

mission. These threats and the news that the pope's legate, John of Casemarino, was now in Bulgaria, caused Basil to return to his native land. Priests and other clerics in his retinue were forbidden to leave Durazzo.[37] Meanwhile, in September, 1203, Basil received the pallium from the hands of the legate.[38]

Shortly after Basil's return from Durazzo, Johannitsa again asked Innocent to send a cardinal empowered "to give him the scepter and the crown." [39] He dispatched the presbyter Constantine and the constable Sergius to the Holy See, enjoining them to inform the pontiff of Basil's misfortune and of Bulgaria's eagerness to embrace the tenets of the Roman Church.[40]

Innocent received the tsar's envoys and prepared to anoint and crown Johannitsa as a faithful son of the "one true Church." Invoking the example of Holy Writ, he once again reminded the tsar of the Church's hegemony over all terrestrial things. As Peter's heir and custodian of the keys of Heaven, Innocent declared himself superior to all people and realms, for God had placed in his hands "the power to destroy and scatter, to implant and erect." [41]

In the fall of 1203, Innocent, saluting Johannitsa as an especially beloved son of the Church, formally placed him and his subjects under the jurisdiction of the Apostolic Chair. The tsar and his nobility were admonished to maintain peace and encourage reform within their realms so that "they might not incur irreparable detriment." [42] After acceding to all of Johannitsa's requests, Innocent invested

[37] Migne (ed.), *P.L.*, CCXV, cols. 155–56.
[38] Guérin-Songéon, *Bulgarie*, 241.
[39] Migne (ed.), *P.L.*, CCXV, cols. 290–91, 292.
[40] *Ibid.*, cols. 155–56.   [41] *Ibid.*, cols. 156–57, 158.
[42] *Ibid.*, col. 158.

Leo, cardinal-presbyter of the Church of the Holy Cross, with legatine powers to anoint the tsar. The pope admonished Johannitsa to accept the royal standard from Leo and to regard it as an emblem of Christ's Church and love. The tsar was also advised to employ his authority with a humble heart; to remember, during the bitterness of war, the Passion of Christ; and to recognize always the sovereignty of Peter's successors.[43]

Establishment of a strong Bulgar Church, free from all Byzantine influences, was one of Johannitsa's paramount objectives. Just before his coronation the tsar, acknowledging the pope as "the master of the whole world," petitioned Innocent "to accomplish the desire of his realm by forwarding a pastoral staff and other accoutrements to which patriarchs are accustomed." Johannitsa requested also that Basil, Archbishop of Tirnova, "first patriarch of Bulgaria," he recognized as primate. Of far greater significance was the tsar's next behest. "I ask," he wrote to Innocent, "that the Roman Church concede to the church of Tirnova the right to elect and consecrate its own patriarch." Innumerable wars and the great distance separating Bulgaria from the Holy See, Johannitsa maintained, rendered impossible their recourse to Rome after the death of each patriarch. In addition, the tsar sought permission to consecrate the Chrism in the church of Tirnova, a privilege denied by the Greeks, who were disgruntled by the Bulgarian submission to the pope.[44]

Innocent granted all of Johannitsa's requests and authorized Cardinal Leo to confer primacy upon the Archbishop of Tirnova. The pope proclaimed Basil both primate and patriarch, with the interesting ruling that these two

---

[43] *Ibid.*, cols. 295–96.   [44] *Ibid.*, cols. 290–91, 292.

titles were synonymous, being distinct names applicable to similar functions and offices. Authority to "bless, anoint, and crown," the successive rulers of Bulgaria was accorded exclusively to the Archbishop of Tirnova and his successors.

Other important prerogatives were conferred upon the province of Tirnova and its patriarch. In a letter to Basil, Innocent enunciated these rights and their formulas: "At the time of your [Basil's] death, no one is to be elevated surreptitiously to the See of Tirnova; rather, only he who has been elected by the canons and suffragans of the church in the approved manner will be recognized. Once chosen, he will send nuncios to the Holy See to request the pallium. . . . In the event of the death of a bishop under your jurisdiction, you will confirm the election of his successor and bestow upon him the archiepiscopal consecration." [45] Minor privileges authorized Basil to consecrate the Chrism, ordain priests, and dedicate new churches in his province.

Comparing the Bulgarian clergy and people to errant sheep returning to their shepherd, Innocent ordered them to "respect as inviolate" the legate Leo, then in Bulgaria to confer pallia, "manifest emblems of full, pontifical power," upon the archbishops of Tirnova and Velesbud.[46] The prelates swore eternal fealty to God, the Virgin Mary, the Apostles, and all of the saints, and to Innocent as Peter's legatee. The solemn oath taken by Basil is especially indicative of his professed subservience to the pope:

> I, Archbishop of Tirnova, primate of all Bulgaria and Walachia, from this hour and ever hereafter, shall be faithful and obedient to the Holy Roman and Apostolic Chair of the Blessed Peter, to my Lord, Innocent III, and his Catholic successors. . . . Rather than err in

[45] *Ibid.*, cols. 280–82.   [46] *Ibid.*, col. 294.

deed, advice, or consent, I would prefer to lose my members, or even my life; and no man will obtain from me any information confided to my secrecy.

I shall defend, with all my power, the Roman Pontiff against all living things. . . . Unless I am prevented by canonical embarrassments, I shall come to synods to which I am summoned; and, unless I am absolved from them, I shall undertake, four times a year, ad limina visits to Rome, or else send nuncios in my place. . . .

. . . .

I shall exact from the King of Bulgaria and Walachia, the coronation of whom is allowed to me by the Apostolic Chair, and all of his subjects, promises of obedience and devotion to the Roman Church. . . . I shall observe all of these things in good faith. . . .[47]

However thorough Basil's oath of obedience to the Holy See was, the extensive rights assigned to him as primate placed him at the head of an almost autocephalous church. Johannitsa had accomplished his purpose, for the rights granted the church of Tirnova served all national needs and, what is more, protected the episcopacy from the power of the Byzantine Empire.

Johannitsa's conflict with the leaders of the Latin Kingdom of Constantinople was a dismal epilogue to the rapport achieved by Bulgaria and the papacy as a result of the tsar's coronation and the important concessions which Innocent granted to the Archbishopric of Tirnova. The pope's efforts to secure Emperor Baldwin's release completely failed, and negotiations for lasting peace between the Latin Kingdom and the Bulgarian Empire, largely inspired by the pope, also came to naught. The Latins, Johannitsa maintained, refused to conclude peace unless part of his empire were ceded to them, terms he spurned on the ground

[47] *Ibid.*, col. 295.

that since he had been crowned with the authority of the pope, the Latins actually were usurpers of his legitimate rights. In 1207 a Turkish boyard, perhaps at the instigation of the tsar's wife, killed him as he lay sleeping in his tent. Shortly before, Innocent had again written to the Bulgarian ruler, requesting that he make peace with the Latins, but with the tsar's death, negotiations between Innocent and the Bulgarian state terminated.[48]

POLAND

The emergence of Poland into the light of European history was associated with the establishment of Roman Catholic Christianity by the conversion of Mesco I in 966 and his marriage to the Catholic Princess Dubravka of Bohemia. Indeed, the conversion of Mesco in its significance for Poland was comparable with that of Clovis for the Kingdom of the Franks. Under Boleslav I (992–1025) an archbisopric was established at Gniezno, and this prelacy henceforth was the real, enduring symbol of Polish unity and its orientation toward the Catholic West. With the concurrence of Emperor Otto III of the Holy Roman Empire, the newly consecrated Polish primate invested Boleslav with the royal crown.[49] With Boleslav's coronation "all the elements which could constitute order, force, and progress were united. . . . The king was the anointed of the Church and the chief of an army of volunteers; the people were called to fulfill the mission of Christian propagation."[50]

Unfortunately the fair prospects incident to the founda-

[48] *Ibid.*, cols. 705–706, 710.

[49] Edouard Krakowski, *Histoire de la Pologne* (Paris, 1934), 38.

[50] Marcellina Skibinska, *La formation de la nationalité Polonaise sous les premiers Piasts au xe et xie siècles* (Toulouse, 1937), 85.

tion of the Piast dynasty were largely unrealized because of the rupture of peace between Poland and the German Empire in the reign of Mesco II (1025–1034). Reconstruction began, however, with the accession of Casimir I, the Restorer (1034–1058); and Boleslav II, the Bold (1058–1079), was able to reconstitute the monarchy with his coronation at Cracow on Christmas Day, 1076. Ties between the Polish state and Roman Catholicism were strengthened by Boleslav's adherence to Pope Gregory VII in the great Investiture Struggle, but this accord was ruptured when Stanislaus, Bishop of Cracow, like Thomas à Becket, was murdered before his altar as the tragic sequel to a quarrel with the king.[51]

With Boleslav's death, the powerful nobles reduced royal authority to impotence; indeed, Sieciech, one of the great Palatines, exercised virtually monarchical powers. Boleslav III, Crooked Mouth (1102–1138), then regained much of the authority forfeited by the crown during the previous chaotic years, and in the Battle of Hundsfeld (1109) recovered Silesia. In an endeavor to ensure greater stability to the government and to avoid internecine strife among members of the Piast family, the king's will provided for the creation of four duchies—Silesia, Mosovia, Great Poland, and Sandomierz. The king's eldest son was to inherit Silesia and Cracow, which was to be inseparably associated with the grand ducal power. Upon his death, in turn, the grand dukedom was to go to the eldest heir of the family branch ruling Mosovia, and so on in rotation.[52] But Poland was too immature politically for federal government, and

---

[51] Oskar Halecki, *A History of Poland* (2d ed.; New York, 1943), 12–20; Clemens Brandenburger, *Pölnische Geschichte* (Leipzig, 1907), 21; Roman Dyboski, *Outlines of Polish History* (2d ed.; London, 1931), 17.

[52] Henri Grappin, *Histoire de la Pologne des origines à 1922* (Paris, 1922), 24–29; Brandenburger, *Pölnische Geschichte*, 22.

the impracticability of the scheme for rotating grand ducal authority was manifest to Casimir II. In 1180 the nobles acknowledged Casimir and his heirs as hereditary lords of Cracow and Grand Dukes of Poland in the Assembly of Lencyca, and this decision received the approbation of both pope and emperor. Disaffection nonetheless continued, and Wladislav, Casimir's successor, won recognition as Grand Duke only after eight years of bitter fighting.[53]

Duke Wladislav was not only the most powerful suzerain in Poland; he was also, from Innocent's viewpoint, the most defiant and contumacious. After having been subjected to a broad canonical sentence subsequent to his imprisonment of the Archbishop of Gniezno,[54] the duke continued to violate the traditional liberties of the Church, moving Innocent to excoriate him as the "son of misery and wrath, the prevaricator of prevaricators, who built damnably against God, like mud in opposition to brick." In order that the duke might determine whether or not he had the power "with which to trample upon the Church of Christ," the pope adjured him "to collect his senses, consider his better nature, mete out his strength, and take count of his virtues."

Oblivious to canonical censures, Wladislav had ordered a convocation of the bishops of his domains and compelled them to confer prebends upon certain of his abettors. In addition, relics, church ornaments, and innumerable objects donated by the faithful were collected and consigned to the custody of the duke. By virtue of the Biblical law "whereby God had granted the care of the ornaments of the Tabernacle to the Levites," these duties, Innocent declared, were the inviolate rights of prelates and chapters.[55]

---

[53] Brandenburger, *Pölnische Geschichte*, 22.   [54] *Supra*, 5–6.
[55] Migne (ed.), *P.L.*, CCXV, cols. 1060–61.

Henry, Archbishop of Gniezno, accordingly was invested with authority to compel obedience from the duke in matters affecting the future welfare of the Church.[56]

In Poland, as in most of western Europe, lay investiture continued to be a thorn in the side of the papacy. Because of "an excess of insolence in certain parts of Poland which raged furiously against the liberties of the Church," Innocent censured those noblemen who "presumed to arrogate to themselves the right of electing priests." Under threat of eternal anathema, all Polish dukes were warned to refrain from the election of priests and canons which exclusively appertained to monastic chapters and prelates. Canons likewise were assured of their freedom to solemnize all such elections.[57]

Another similar missive deplored the ducal practice of filling vacant church offices and prebends. Reminding the dukes that "they held all earthly possessions from Him who inhabits Heaven," the pope reproved them for "presuming to wander in certain provinces wherein they deprived the churches of what was owed them and transgressed upon priestly powers." Innocent prohibited such practices and urged the nobles to defer in all matters to the churches, "so that they might in time come to revere them." [58]

When a certain Paul, "unable to retain in mind the example of Judas," was nominated and elected Bishop of Posen by secular princes, the Archbishop of Gniezno rejected his qualifications and subjected him to an interdict. The bishop, however, continued to persecute the Church and even presumed to celebrate the Divine Office. Because of this offense he was anathematized by the archbishop, whom Innocent,

[56] *Ibid.*, col. 1066.   [57] *Ibid.*, cols. 1064–65.
[58] *Ibid.*, cols. 1071–72.

"prescribing like punishments for like excesses," authorized to proceed with equal rigor against all other similarly recalcitrant prelates.[59]

The spoliation of church goods by laymen throughout the Polish duchies evoked the pope's repeated reprobation. Laymen, "shunning the just order of things," had divested churches and clerics of both movable and immovable properties bordering upon their own patrimonies. Berating the secular princes' inconsideration for the Church, the Holy Father drew an analogy between their malversation and the liberty and respect allowed the Israelites while they lived in bondage under Pharoah. For the latter, although he walked in darkness, had permitted the Jews to retain their original liberty and, honoring their priests and Levites, had allowed them to minister spiritual nourishment to their people. Polish princes, on the other hand, exacted heavy and disturbing payments from their priests. Further construing these "lay oppressions against churchmen as the resistance of insolence," Innocent commanded all bishops in Poland to prohibit—if necessary, by means of canonical censure—the continued confiscation of church possessions.[60]

On rare occasions, a Polish duke or lord would merit papal approval. One such notable instance was the case of the Duke of Cracow; [61] another involved Ladislaus, the son of Odo, former claimant of the Grand Duchy. Both of these princes, because of their sincere devotion to the Church and its liberties, were placed under the aegis of the successors of "the Apostle, Blessed Peter." [62] All of their possessions were likewise accorded papal protection from molestation by other claimants.[63] In return for such papal

[59] *Ibid.*, cols. 1066–67.
[61] *Ibid.*, col. 1067.
[63] *Ibid.*, CCXV, col. 1067.
[60] *Ibid.*, cols. 1067–68.
[62] *Ibid.*, CCXVI, col. 416–17.

patronage, Ladislaus was directed to donate, once every three years, a stipulated offering to the Apostolic Chair.[64]

Indifference, and sometimes recalcitrance, characterized the attitude of the Polish nobility and people toward the payment of church tithes. Innocent counseled all of the faithful in Poland to pay promptly any assessments owed to the Holy See. Attempts to defraud the Apostolic Chair, Innocent admonished, might result in the subjection of the guilty ones to the "terrible vengeance" visited upon Ananias and Sapphira, who, because they withheld certain monies from the first Apostolic community, fell dead while kneeling repentantly at the feet of Simon Peter. All Christians, consequently, were ordered expressly to pay sums rightfully claimed by the pope.[65]

Dukes of the kingdom were exhorted to pay tenths, "the first fruits of the Lord," to their respective churches, and Innocent condemned those who had absolved devoted vassals from the payment of tenths. "You think little," he wrote to the dukes, "of injury to God, because He endures, sustains, and does not openly repel your attack. Lest, indeed, the Lord become angry with you and punish you for all of your injuries to Him at once, the Apostolic Chair adjures and orders you to desist from such temerity. . . ." The pontiff stressed that the dukes were "not to impede, or cause otherwise to be impeded," the punctual payment of tithes.[66] The nobility were also ordered to accommodate and shelter visiting priests and archdeacons, and to provide them with donations for the cathedrals to which they were attached.[67]

One of the few letters in which Innocent literally exulted dealt with the conversion of pagans living in Prussia, then

[64] *Ibid.*, CCXVI, col. 416.   [65] *Ibid.*, CCXV, col. 1063.
[66] *Ibid.*, cols. 1063-64.   [67] *Ibid.*, col. 1064-65.

an appanage of the Polish Grand Duke. The pope likened evangelization to a continuation of the work of "the Farmer of Heaven, Jesus Christ, who had endowed His chosen vine with true life and fertility." All new churches were as palms, germinating from the original root planted by Christ. "Strive to extend holy conversion," Innocent instructed the Archbishop of Gniezno, "by means of good works, not merely for the sake of increasing internal grace, but for the fructification of things recently begun." The pope then spoke with enthusiasm of "Philip, our beloved son in Christ, and other monks of eager and pious desires who, laboring for the vine and wishing to give love to all so that none might perish, have gone, with our permission and in spiritual meekness, to parts of Prussia; [and these men], planting the seed of God's word, have restored to the Truth the infidels dwelling in ignorance and darkness."

Continuing his analogy, Innocent compared the proselytes to seeds sowed in fertile land, which, in season, would bear fruit. He added, however, that new converts, like new plants, required the help of "irrigation"; consequently, all monks and brothers in Prussia were commanded to persevere in the task of conversion so that by the offices of conscientious pastors dissemination of the Christian religion might be aided.[68]

A subsequent letter reflected Innocent's sincere solicitude for the new converts. Apprehensive lest the Polish nobility abuse the nascent Christians, he adjured the dukes to be charitable to them. Faith alone, the pope believed, was not sufficient to satisfy God, for charity was especially necessary. "Because God commanded all to extend love even to enemies," the pope urged the nobles to regard with special

[68] *Ibid.*, CCXVI, cols. 315–16.

charity those people "who recently had forsaken the error of the Gentiles for the Truth, which is Christ." Love, rather than inhuman treatment, would enable the new converts to see the Faith in its true light.

Certain Polish lords, however, preferring "temporal conveniences to the praises of angels," aggravated the condition of the Prussian converts by subjecting them to undue hardships and placing "innumerable impediments in their way." Hence, the pope reasoned, "those who have received recently the liberty of the Christian Faith are in reality more oppressed than they were formerly under the yoke of their pristine servitude." All nobles were enjoined to refrain from the continued aggravation of these new converts, "who, with so little divine mercy, might relapse easily into the error of their former ways." Instead, they were exhorted to recall Christ, "Who had come to make salvation possible and Who had died for the redemption of all." [69]

The task of promulgating and enforcing Innocent's pronouncements affecting Poland usually devolved upon Henry Kietlicz, Archbishop of Gniezno and former classmate of the pope during their university days.[70] As primate of Poland he was invested with the right to bear the crucifix in all important religious processions in the province of Gniezno. Only the papal legate to Poland, inasmuch as he proceeded "from the side of the pope," could precede the archbishop in demonstrations or pageants of a religious character.[71]

[69] *Ibid.*, col. 670.
[70] Brandenburger, *Pölnische Geschichte*, 22.
[71] Migne (ed.), *P.L.*, CCXV, col. 1073.

Execution of the canonical sentence imposed upon the contumacious Wladislav was entrusted to the Archbishop of Gniezno. In the event of repentance and expiation on the part of the Duke, Henry was authorized to grant him absolution in accordance with the customary formulas of the Church.[72] In addition, Innocent, convinced of the archbishop's prudence, adjured him to compel Wladislav and his supporters to restore to him all liberties and immunities incident to the integrity of the Church in Poland. The archbishop simultaneously was authorized to revoke prebends and offices conferred upon persons hostile to the Church during the reign of Wladislav's father. This privilege comprehended the right to alienate the possessions of men "who had menaced the Church in defiance of its head." [73]

Still another directive to Archbishop Henry confirmed his spiritual supremacy over the three most powerful dukes in Poland, Lesco, Conrad, and Wladislav. Comparing the Church to the Bride of Christ, "preserved without blemish or wrinkle," Innocent counseled the archbishop "to strengthen those statutes relating to us and to the conservation of the privileges of the Church." The aforenamed dukes were forbidden to confiscate the gold, silver, costly vestments, or palfreys of bishops who had died intestate; rather, they were ordered to assign all such possessions in their entirety to the church of the deceased bishop.[74]

Instructions to the Polish clergy relevant to their submission to the Archbishop of Gniezno in matters pertaining to the welfare of the Church attest to the high esteem in which he was held by the Holy Father. All bishops were directed to think solicitiously of the primate and to pro-

[72] *Ibid.*, col. 1059.　　　　[73] *Ibid.*, col. 1066.
[74] *Ibid.*, CCXVI, cols. 412–13.

vide him with "triumphant and militant aids." [75] Sigwino, Bishop of Pomerania, was reprimanded severely for his hesitation in manifesting proper obedience and respect to Henry.[76] Innocent did not stint his laudation of Henry, "who, through many anxieties and dangers, labored and continued to labor, not only for the general peace, but for the liberties of the Church as well." [77]

[75] *Ibid.*, CCXV, col. 1068.   [76] *Ibid.*, col. 1069.
[77] *Ibid.*, col. 1068.

CHAPTER VII

CRUSADING PLANS, 1204–1216

D URING the eighteen years of his reign the most absorbing thought of Innocent, the purpose to which he most constantly adhered, was the deliverance of the Holy Land"; [1] indeed, "there was a fundamental agreement between the pope's duty to save the Holy Land and his claim to universal domination." [2] After the Fourth Crusade had been diverted by the Venetians to the capture of Zara, Innocent ordered the crusading leaders to abstain from involvement in the affairs of the Eastern Empire lest they aggravate the sin committed against the Hungarian city by another attack on Christians. [3] Yet his orders were defied, and he was confronted by a *fait accompli* with the capture of Constantinople and the election of Baldwin as emperor. Difficulties in reorganizing the crusade were aggravated by Innocent's refusal to compromise his reform ideals for the attainment of this paramount objective. Efforts of the Venetians to dominate the patriarchate of Constantinople and its enormous ecclesiastical patronage, the imprisonment of the Patriarch of Antioch, and the seizure of Templar properties by secular princes were only a few of the problems involved in the larger task of reviving the crusade.

[1] Edward Pears, *The Fall of Constantinople* (New York, 1886), 231.

[2] P. A. Throop, *Criticism of the Crusade: A Study of Public Opinion and Crusade Propaganda* (Amsterdam, 1940), 3.

[3] Migne (ed.), *P.L.*, CCXV, cols. 106–107.

Yet it could be plausibly maintained that the organization of the Latin Empire in the East constituted an important preliminary to the eventual attack on the Saracens, either in Egypt or in Syria. Villehardouin, who expressed the viewpoint of the crusading leaders, sincerely believed that this was the case,[4] and Innocent "at first had faith in the solidity of the Latin conquest and believed that Constantinople would become the center for the organization of the crusade, the rallying point necessary for Christian conquests in the East." [5] In reply to Baldwin, who informed him of his election and emphasized the advantages of the tenure of Constantinople, the pope expressed satisfaction that the Greeks had been "changed by the righteous judgment of God from pride to humility, from disobedience to devotion, from a kingdom of schismatics to one of Catholics." [6] He declared that "to all, both clergy and lay crusaders in the Christian army, in the hope of remission of sins and the indulgences which the Apostolic See promised them, we enjoin and order, for the defense and retention of the Empire of Constantinople, *by aid of which the Holy Land can be more easily liberated from the hands of the pagans,* that they assist you prudently and powerfully." [7]

[4] Jean Longnon, *Le Français d'outre mer* (Paris, 1929), 202. Georgius Acropolita, "Chronicle of Constantinople," in *Historiens Grecs* (4 vols.) I, 566, of *Recueil des historiens des croisades,* 16 vols. (Paris, 1841–1906), viewed the conquest as an opportunity to end dangerous dissension in the empire. See also "De Syria Expugnata," in *Historiens Grecs,* I, 602, *ibid.*

[5] Louis Brehier, *L'église et l'orient au moyen âge* (3d ed.; Paris, 1911), 171.

[6] Migne (ed.), *P.L.,* CCXV, cols. 454–55. See his letter to Dandalo, *ibid.,* 511–12.

[7] Migne (ed.), *P.L.,* CCXV, cols. 454–55. Italics mine. Baldwin naturally minimized the part played by the Venetians in reporting the events at Constantinople. Ernst Gerland, *Geschichte des lateinischen Kaiserreiches von Konstantinopel: Geschichte der Kaiser Baldwin I und Heinrich I 1204–1216* (Hamburg, 1905), 11–12.

In May, 1205, in a letter addressed to all the clergy and people of Constantinople, Innocent declared that "the Lord had deigned to open a way for the recovery of His land by the miraculous transfer of the Empire from the Greeks to the Latins." All were admonished to aid in strengthening the newly won empire in its devotion to the Holy See during the ensuing year.[8]

The tenacity with which the pope clung to the hope that the crusade might be resumed is also shown by his attitude toward the election of Thomas Morosini as Patriarch of Constantinople. When the pontiff officially was informed of the choice by Enrico Dandalo, Doge of Venice, he pointed out that it was irregular, since lay influences had been predominant. Yet, despite his strong feelings in the matter, he informed the doge that he concurred in the election in the belief that his approval would strengthen the resolution of the Venetians to co-operate in the resumption of the crusade.[9] He also expressed this attitude in his letter which announced the confirmation of Thomas to Baldwin,[10] as well as in a letter to Thomas himself.[11]

The pope was much concerned with the reorganization of the Eastern Church. As he explained to Baldwin in May, 1205, the empire was the vineyard which the Lord had put in the keeping of new husbandmen. It was a source of profound satisfaction that, just as the cloak of Christ had

[8] Delisle (ed.), "Lettres inédites d'Innocent III," *loc. cit.*, 408–409.

[9] Migne (ed.), *P.L.*, CCXV, cols. 512–17. It is strange that this point should have been completely ignored by Ludwig Streit, *Beiträge zur Geschichte des vierten Kreuzzüges* (Anklam, 1877), 33.

[10] Migne (ed.), *P.L.*, CCXV, col. 517. At Rome Thomas was elevated in successive ceremonies from subdeacon to bishop and then confirmed as archbishop. "Gesta" in Migne (ed.), *P.L.*, CCXIV, cols. xcviii–xcxix. See also Potthast (ed.), *Regesta*, I, No. 2466.

[11] Delisle (ed.), "Lettres inédites d'Innocent III," *loc. cit.*, 409–410.

remained whole when His vestments were divided at the crucifixion, so the Church which He had put on as a cloak had been united as a result of the capture of Constantinople.[12] Nevertheless, the pope's letters show no abatement of his efforts to ensure revival of the crusade. The Bishop of Soissons was commissioned for three years as a papal legate in Constantinople to collaborate with Baldwin to advance the crusading plans.[13] In a general letter to the clergy and people of Constantinople the pope ordered them to give assistance and counsel to the emperor to hasten the recovery of the Holy Land.[14] Letters to a number of French bishops directed them to urge the clergy and laity of their dioceses to go to Constantinople or to send funds to the emperor "for the defeat of the barbarian peoples who hold the land in which God was king before our age" so that the work auspiciously begun by the capture of the Greek capital might be carried to a glorious culmination.[15]

A few months later the pope addressed all of the faithful who were working for the cause of the Holy Land. He again expressed the view that "by means of the occupancy of the Empire of Constantinople, conquered by divine judgment, it is hoped that Jerusalem can be freed from the pagans," and, therefore, "whoever sighs for the liberation of Jerusalem ought efficaciously to endeavor to strengthen the tenure of Constantinople." Christians who went to the imperial capital were directed to continue their labors for the recovery of Palestine. If they were unable to secure passage from Constantinople, or if they had exhausted their financial resources while awaiting transportation, the pope directed that they inform him by nuncios. He also

---

[12] Migne (ed.), *P.L.*, CCXV, cols. 636–37. [13] *Ibid.*, col. 638.
[14] *Ibid.*, col. 629. [15] *Ibid.*, cols. 634–36.

stated that, if necessary, he was prepared to send transportation from Brindisi.[16]

The pope successfully urged Albert, former Bishop of Vercelli, whom he had prevailed upon to accept the election as Patriarch of Jerusalem early in 1203, to proceed from Constantinople to Syria.[17] A considerable sum was placed at his disposal by the pope "to accompany him on the ardors of his journey which he had begun for the aid of the Lord," [18] and he was granted authority to permit excommunicated persons to join him unless they had sinned so grievously as to warrant submission of their cases to the Apostolic See.[19] Clergy who accompanied Albert were assured tenure of their European benefices for three years.[20]

Despite the pope's efforts, there was little reason for optimism. The famous agreement concluded between the French and Venetians after the capture of Constantinople provided for the division of ecclesiastical benefices. Innocent bitterly condemned this clause of the treaty and forbade Baldwin to carry out the provisions for the assignment of church properties.[21] Equally strong objections were communicated to the doge, who was warned "not to attempt to proceed with the division of church properties nor to permit others to do so." [22]

A more serious matter was the Venetian request to release the crusaders from their vows. The pope, in his letter to the doge, declared that he would not hear of such con-

---

[16] *Ibid.*, col. 706. [17] *Ibid.*, col. 670.
[18] *Ibid.*, col. 753. [19] *Ibid.*, col. 752.
[20] *Ibid.*, col. 670. Albert remained in office until September, 1213. Potthast (ed.), *Regesta*, I, No. 4953. He was authorized to settle a number of disputes that threatened to impair the work of the crusaders. Migne (ed.), *P.L.*, CCXV, cols. 829–30, 863, 1083.
[21] Migne (ed.), *P.L.*, CCXV, cols. 521–22. [22] *Ibid.*, cols. 522–23.

cessions: they would place the papacy in a position where subsequent dissolution of the crusading army could be attributed to remissness on its part.[23] The disposition to consider the crusade ended doubtless was primarily the result of the unauthorized action of Peter of Capua, the pope's Syrian legate, who had "left the land which the Lord sanctified by His presence and in which the mystery of our redemption was consummated" to come to Constantinople, where he absolved the Crusaders from their vows.[24]

News of the Christian capture of Constantinople had precipitated the formation of a powerful Mohammedan coalition, headed by Sophidinius, ruler of Damascus and Egypt. Innocent feared that his legate's defection in the face of this threat would encourage the Saracens to attack parts of the Holy Land still under Christian control, and there was also danger that the Greeks might attempt to recover their capital. He bitterly condemned Peter's attempted termination of the crusade and appealed to King Philip Augustus of France, "whom God had exalted and magnified among all Christian princes," to aid the desperate Christian cause in the East.[25]

Papal misgivings proved to be amply justified. In June, 1205, Henry, brother of Baldwin, reported the startling news that the emperor had been captured by Johannitsa, King of Bulgaria and Walachia, while besieging Adrianople in a campaign to suppress a Greek rebellion. Henry ex-

---

[23] *Ibid.*, cols. 519–21.

[24] *Ibid.*, col. 699. Soffredus had left in 1209. Heinrich Zimmermann, *Die päpstliche Legaten in der ersten Hälfte des 13 Jahrhunderts* (Paderborn, 1913), 53–54. Peter was finally back in Rome in 1207. Benedict of St. Susanna was sent as a legate to Constantinople in May, 1205. Benedict's appointment was announced in April, 1205. Delisle (ed.), "Lettres inédites d'Innocent III," *loc. cit.*, 406–407.

[25] Migne (ed.), *P.L.*, CCXV, cols. 698–99.

pressed fear that this disaster would result in the creation of an alliance of Greeks, Saracens, and Bulgars that would jeopardize Christian occupation of Constantinople. He besought the pope for aid, emphasizing the fact that the Templars and Hospitalers shared his conviction that liberation of Baldwin was a paramount necessity.[26]

Innocent responded to his appeal by insisting that establishment of peace between the empire and his protégé, the Bulgarian king, should be a necessary concomitant of efforts for the emperor's release.[27] He also wrote to Johannitsa, urging him to free the captive emperor and hinting that failure to do so might result in the formation of an alliance between the empire and his enemy, the King of Hungary.[28]

Johannitsa replied that he would not release Baldwin until territories that had been seized from him by the empire were returned.[29] He maintained that he had been crowned by papal authority,[30] and right was on his side in his struggle with those who "bore false crosses on their shoulders." The impasse continued until the emperor either died or, more probably, was killed in captivity.[31] A subsequent letter from Henry to the pope reported successful Christian counterattacks against the Greek rebels and their

[26] *Ibid.*, CCXVII, cols. 292–94.

[27] *Ibid.*, CCXV, col. 710. Johannitsa, in 1204, had been granted royal insignia by the papal legate, Leo Brancales, Zimmermann, *Päpstliche Legaten*, 36. Baldwin's repudiation of Johannitsa's offer of friendship was a tragic blunder. This is admitted by J. N. Brischar, *Papst Innozenz III und Seine Zeit* (Freiburg, 1883), 270–71, despite his admiration for the emperor.

[28] Migne (ed.), *P.L.*, CCXV, col. 705.

[29] "Gesta," *ibid.*, CCXIV, col. lxxiii.

[30] Migne (ed.), *P.L.*, CCXV, cols. 277–80.

[31] "Gesta," *ibid.*, CCXIV, col. cviii. Nicetas Acominatus, "History of the Byzantine Empire," in *Historiens Grecs*, I, 498, of *Recueil des historiens des croisades*, reports that he was mutilated prior to execution.

confederates, but a Latin garrison stationed at Rossa was virtually annihilated.[32]

Meanwhile, an appreciable number of crusaders under the leadership of the Bishop of Soissons gathered at Genoa to aid the hard-pressed empire in response to the pope's appeal. They reported that they encountered difficulty in securing passage. In December, 1206, in reply to a request for aid the pope suggested that the crusaders embark from Genoa if ships could be secured. In the event they believed that they could proceed more expeditiously from Brindisi, the pontiff assured them of safe conduct to that port and of his willingness to impart his personal blessing if they visited Rome en route.[33] In a letter of the same date to the barons in this crusading group, Innocent informed them that Baldwin had died in captivity, but that Henry, even before his coronation as emperor, had gained some victories over the barbarians that augured well for the success of their relief expedition.[34]

The tremendous difficulties under which the pope labored were shown further by his subsequent relations with Henry. The pontiff reminded the newly crowned emperor that Constantinople had been taken *primarily to expedite aid to the Holy Land;* yet he seemed indifferent to the crusading cause. Indeed, he impeded the project by seizing possessions of the Templars and ignoring papal orders for their return.[35] He also incurred Innocent's wrath by forbidding gifts or bequests to the Church [36] and illegally holding Church properties. On numerous occasions the pope vainly ordered him to return ecclesiastical properties ille-

---

[32] Migne (ed.), *P.L.*, CCXVII, cols. 294–95.
[33] *Ibid.*, CCXV, col. 1036–38.   [34] *Ibid.*
[35] *Ibid.*, CCXIV, cols. 324, 470.   [36] *Ibid.*, CCXVI, col. 296.

gally in his possession and to rescind the prohibition of gifts to the Church.[37] In fairness to Henry, it must be acknowledged that he could have done little to help the crusaders. His struggles with the Bulgars and with Theodore Lascaris, who was crowned King of Nicaea in 1206, precluded participation in crusading activities.[38] It is equally clear that Henry's professions of obedience to the pope meant little or nothing and that he was resolved to curb the wealth and power of the Church in his empire.[39]

Papal relations with Venice remained uneasy. In August, 1206, Innocent refused to grant the Venetian request for the bestowal of the pallium on the newly elected Archbishop of Zara and utilized the occasion again to express his disapproval of the seizure of that city from Hungary. He declared that he maintained discreet silence about Venetian excesses in Constantinople, for the capture of that city promised to make possible the occupation of Egypt and a successful invasion of the Holy Land.[40] In July, 1209, he reiterated his refusal to countenance the elevation of a Venetian to the position of Archbishop of Zara, in a letter to the new doge, Peter Ziano.[41]

Innocent had other reasons for displeasure with the Venetian government. Pilgrims to the Holy Land had been

---

[37] *Ibid.*, cols. 296–97. See also cols. 303, 304, 310–13, 323, 595, 596, 597, 1349. For further statement of difficulties in protecting clergy, see William Miller, *Essays on the Latin Orient* (Cambridge, 1921), 78.

[38] Brehier, *L'église et l'orient au moyen âge*, 173–74. His power remained centered in Nicaea, as stated by Georgius Acropolita, "Chronicle of Constantinople," in *Historiens Grecs*, I, 567–70, of *Recueil des historiens des croisades*.

[39] Achille Luchaire, *Innocent III*, 6 vols. (2d ed.; Paris, 1911), IV, 186–88.

[40] Migne (ed.), *P.L.*, CCXV, cols. 957–59.

[41] *Ibid.*, CCXVI, cols. 88–89.

persuaded to go to Greece or Crete to serve Venetian interests on the promise that they were eligible to receive the
same indulgences that were granted to those who visited
the Holy Land. The doge and people of Venice were ordered to abstain from this pernicious practice "lest they
offend God more than they are known already to have
offended Him." Fighting against Christians in Crete or
elsewhere was forbidden, and unless the Venetians made
prompt amends for their misconduct, they were threatened
with excommunication.[42] They were also warned to desist
from their efforts to curtail legacies to the Church,[43] and
their interference in the affairs of the church of Durazzo
likewise was condemned.[44]

Success of the pope's plan to use the Eastern Empire as a
base for the crusade he so ardently desired naturally depended to a considerable degree on the co-operation of the
Patriarch of Constantinople. Unfortunately, until Thomas'
death in 1211, Innocent was involved in controversy with
him. The chief cause of papal vexation was the question
of appointments to the canonries of the Church of St. Sophia.
Shortly after election to the patriarchal chair, Thomas concluded an agreement with the Venetians to reserve these
positions for them. Innocent promptly nullified this arrangement and forbade its observance under pain of anathema,[45] but his orders were virtually disregarded.[46]

The patriarch, to be sure, presented a different version
of his policies. He claimed, apparently truthfully, that
the agreement in respect to the canonries had been extorted
while he tarried in Venice on his way from Rome to Con-

[42] *Ibid.*, cols. 11–12.
[43] *Ibid.*, CCXV, col. 1349.
[44] *Ibid.*, CCXVI, cols. 105–106.
[45] *Ibid.*, CCXV, cols. 947–48.
[46] *Ibid.*, cols. 914–15.

stantinople. He further maintained that he disavowed his commitments to the Venetians immediately after arrival in Constantinople, and his subsequent assignments of the St. Sophia prebends therefore were not made in conformity with any obligations incurred at Venice.[47]

Innocent nonetheless continued to cast strictures on the patriarch's partiality for Venetians, which he displayed not only in the installation of canons but also in the disposition of even more important ecclesiastical positions. The primate was reminded that he was the spiritual father of many children, and therefore committed a grievous sin in reserving his favors for the Venetians. He was ordered to install in the canonries only such candidates as were approved by the papal legate in Constantinople, on pain of suspension if he failed to comply with the papal mandates.[48] The patriarch yielded only partial and grudging obedience to the pontiff's orders and further complicated the problem of patronage by quarreling with Emperor Henry over the disposition of the St. Sophia canonries and other church offices.[49]

Bitterness between the French and Venetians flared up openly after the patriarch's death in 1211. When the suffragans assembled to elect his successor, the Venetians seized the cathedral stalls and, with threats of violence against dissenters, elected the dean of the chapter to the patriarchal chair. Non-Venetian canons chose three candidates whose names they submitted to the pope. Innocent quashed the election and directed the canons to hold a valid one in accordance with prescribed procedure, but he eventually found it necessary to provide an incumbent.[50]

[47] *Ibid.*, CCXVI, cols. 118–23, 162.
[48] *Ibid.*, cols. 117, 218–19, 1387–92.
[49] *Ibid.*, CCXVI, cols. 147–48.　　　　[50] *Ibid.*, cols. 459–60.

The tenor of the pope's correspondence in regard to the resumption of the crusade indicates that he preferred a direct expedition to Syria. It therefore was all the more discouraging when implacable enmities were aroused concerning control of Antioch. Leo, King of Armenia, laid claim to the city in behalf of his grandnephew Rupend, while Bohemond, Count of Tripoli, refused to relinquish his alleged rights. The quarrel was aggravated by the fact that the Templars sided with the king, whereas the Hospitalers espoused the count's cause.[51]

In February, 1207, Bohemond imprisoned the Patriarch of Antioch. The pope immediately ordered Albert of Jerusalem to secure his release and to settle the dispute between the count and the Armenian king which in large measure was responsible for the outrage.[52] But the situation in Antioch was more complicated than appeared on the surface. The patriarch had appointed a relative, who was below the legal minimum age, to a canonry, despite the prohibition of the papal legate. When tension mounted over this issue, a mob attacked the patriarch and threatened to supersede him with a Greek. The fact that a considerable portion of the populace were in open rebellion against their ecclesiastical head doubtless encouraged the count to attack him.[53]

Hopes for a satisfactory settlement of the affair were dashed by the death of the imprisoned patriarch. "O noble Antioch," wrote the pope, "may you realize how gravely

---

[51] *Ibid.*, CCXV, cols. 555–57, 558–59, 698–99; CCXVI, cols. 54–55. Sempad, in his "Armenian Chronicle," states that many of the nobles of the city favored Leo. *Documents Armeniens* (4 vols.), I, 643, of *Recueil des historiens des croisades;* see also Vahram of Edessa, "Rimed Chronicle of Armenia," *Documents Armeniens*, I, 512, *ibid.*

[52] Migne (ed.), *P.L.*, CCXV, cols. 1321–23.

[53] *Ibid.*, cols. 1278–82.

you have been traduced by so heinous a crime." He denounced the sacrilege committed by Bohemond, whom he ordered excommunicated and anathematized. The Patriarch of Jerusalem was directed to supervise a speedy election of a new incumbent of the Antiochan see and was authorized to act as papal vice-regent in all matters pertaining to the Syrian metropolis.[54]

The count remained unchastened. With his active encouragement the disgruntled populace of Antioch attempted to install a Greek patriarch, as they had threatened to do sometime before, and the pope excoriated those whom he considered responsible for this "bold rebellion." [55] Fortunately, in March, 1209, the election of Peter, Bishop of Cyprus, to the vacant prelacy restored order, and Innocent expressed deep satisfaction that a major obstacle to his plans for a crusade had thus been surmounted.[56]

The Armenian king still was contumacious, however, and his strife with the Count of Tripoli and his Templar allies was exacerbated by seizure of Templar properties.[57] Innocent ordered the excommunication of the king and personally exhorted him to make peace, while, at the same time, similar punishment of the Templars was threatened if they refused to accept an equitable adjustment of the case.[58] In June, 1209, the pope repeated his admonitions to Leo. A serious aspect of the situation was the fact that troops were being used in internecine strife which could have been employed to advantage against the Saracens,[59] but it was not until four years later that the king expressed

[54] *Ibid.*, cols. 1428–29. For additional references, see Reinhold Röhrricht, *Regesta Regni Hierosolymitani* (Berlin, 1893), 214, n. 1.

[55] Migne (ed.), *P.L.*, CCXV, col. 1427.

[56] *Ibid.*, CCXVI, cols. 18–19, 46–47, 48.   [57] *Ibid.*, cols. 430–32.

[58] *Ibid.*, cols. 18–19.   [59] *Ibid.*, cols. 54–56.

willingness to compose his quarrels with the Templars. Innocent agreed to his absolution but in view of the enormity of the offenses refused to have his claims to Antioch considered.[60]

These major problems, to say nothing of lesser but nonetheless vexatious matters such as the strife between the King of Cyprus and his constable,[61] did not cause the pope to deviate from his cherished crusading objective. In the letters which he wrote in response to these discouraging manifestations of avarice and jealousy, he insisted upon the necessity for unity in the Christian world lest internecine quarrels vitiate strength which should be turned against the Saracens, and his efforts to arouse and sustain crusading fervor continued.

In March, 1207, he encouraged pledged crusaders in Rome "to place all their hopes in God since He, while you fear Him, converts the plans of the enemies of Christ's Cross into darkness and danger, and, in addition to granting eternal glory, will change present adversities to prosperity." The pope promised that a multitude would soon come to their aid, "with whom they would be able to labor diligently and efficiently for the expulsion of the pagans from the boundaries of Christian territories with God's help." [62] Pledged crusaders who wished to be released from their vows, or to have them commuted, found the pontiff reluctant to make concessions unless adequate guarantees were secured to ensure subsequent fulfillment of their vows.[63]

When the Bishop of Soissons complained that tournaments impeded his efforts to organize a group of crusaders,

[60] Ibid., cols. 792–93.　　[61] Ibid., cols. 46–47, 48, 466.
[62] Ibid., CCXV, cols. 1131–32.
[63] Ibid., cols. 1085, 1136–37, 1174; Potthast (ed.), Regesta, I, No. 1346.

the pope, in June, 1207, declared that he had no intention to condone tournaments, which were known to be forbidden by the Scriptures. Yet he considered inexpedient the bishop's action in excommunicating participants in tournaments, since in protest against the bishop's severity many knights had refused to take the cross or to fulfill vows already taken. He directed the prelate to lift the excommunications and expressed gratitude for the sums which certain knights had promised to dedicate to the crusade after their absolution.[64]

The plight of the Christian captives held as slaves in Alexandria also grieved the pontiff and strengthened his determination to organize a crusade. The Patriarch of Alexandria, who, "placed in the midst of a depraved and perverse nation, emitted the odor of devotion like a lily among thorns," [65] reported that the sufferings of the captives created the danger that they would renounce their faith. The pope exhorted the patriarch to attempt to convince these unfortunates that they underwent temporary tribulations which should be easy to bear in view of the eternal awards that awaited them.[66] At the same time, he urged the Patriarch of Jerusalem to take all possible measures to hasten the liberation of the captives and authorized him to draw upon church properties to finance such efforts.[67]

By 1208 the pontiff's plans for a crusade began to assume more tangible form with the announcement of Leopold of Austria's intention to lead an expedition to the Holy Land. In February of that year the pope praised Leopold's pious resolution; for, "recognizing with a religious mind that he should return recompense to the Lord for all things bestowed on him, he planned humbly to imitate Christ,

---

[64] Migne (ed.), *P.L.*, CCXV, cols. 1174–75.   [65] *Ibid.*, CCXVI, col. 23.
[66] *Ibid.*, cols. 506–507.   [67] *Ibid.*, cols. 507–509.

who, for him, was made obedient even unto death—the death of the cross." Yet what the duke promised to do was little in comparison with what the Redeemer had done for him. He was taking up a light cross, whereas the Lord had borne a heavy one. The duke had sewed a cross upon his garments with thread; the Lord had been affixed to His cross by hard, iron nails.[68] About a month later Leopold, his family, and his properties were placed under the special protection of the Apostolic See.[69]

The pope subsequently informed the grand masters of the Templars and Hospitalers that a large army was being prepared under Leopold's direction, while forces likewise were gathering in France. German princes instituted a general collection for the financial support of Leopold's enterprise, and the pontiff hastened to take further steps to ensure adequate financing of the project by dedicating a fortieth from the Cistercian Order and £1,000 Provence to be expended at the discretion of the officials of the crusading orders. The masters were ordered to be constant and solicitous in their government of Antioch, Tripoli, and such other parts of the East as still were in Christian possession, until the armies now being mobilized could come to their assistance.[70]

In December the pope wrote a strong letter of exhortation to all Christians in Lombardy. He wished that he could better explain, and they could more fully realize, the enormity of their sin in remaining indifferent to the plight of the Holy Land. What would a temporal king do

[68] *Ibid.*, CCXV, cols. 1339–41. Walter Norden, *Das Papsttum und Byzanz* (Berlin, 1903), 176, 180, claims the pope abandoned his plan to continue the crusade from Constantinople by the end of 1207. There is no evidence in the letters to support this view.

[69] Migne (ed.), *P.L.*, CCXV, col. 1341.   [70] *Ibid.*, cols. 1427–28.

to faithless and improvident servants who not only were
responsible for the loss of his kingdom but also refused to
aid in efforts for its recovery? How much greater guilt was
incurred when Christ "was driven out of the land which He
secured by the price of His blood, not by His fault but
theirs, and they neglected to aid Him to recover it?" Some
might say that God who darkened the heavens and rent
the veil of the temple during the crucifixion could save the
land Himself. But God's knowledge is not mere experience
—He knows all eternally and therefore permitted the land,
sanctified by the blood of Christ, to fall into the hands of
the infidels in order to give Christians an opportunity to
serve Him by their efforts for its recovery.[71]

All able to bear arms were exhorted to take the cross,
while others were admonished to contribute funds to defray
expenses. No one was to excuse himself on the ground that
his contribution was too small. Indulgences and forgiveness
of sins were promised to those who went at the expense of
others or sent substitutes. Persons and goods were received
under papal protection, oaths to pay usury were nullified,
and works of penance were commuted to almsgiving for the
crusade.[72]

New emphasis was given to the crusading project with
the marriage of John, Count of Brienne, to Mary, heiress
of the Kingdom of Jerusalem. Since the count was a vassal
of Philip Augustus, who had been instrumental in arrang-
ing the marriage, the pope hastened to urge the French
king to lend aid in the project to secure the throne for him.
Some of the king's advisers claimed that participation in
the crusade would leave France stripped of power and resources. The pope, in his letter of May, 1209, refuted these

[71] *Ibid.*, cols. 1500–1503.   [72] *Ibid.*

contentions and insisted that greater strength and prosperity would redound to the kingdom in the event of a successful crusade in which the king collaborated. Philip accordingly was exhorted to help John as much as possible, and the pope declared that he would set an example by allocating 1400 marks to the count to be disbursed by officials of the crusading orders in consultation with the Patriarch of Jerusalem.[73]

Great events forced a temporary curtailment of the pope's activities to promote a crusade. The murder of Peter Castelnau, Innocent's legate in Toulouse, precipitated the Albigensian crusade and enlisted the services of many knights who otherwise might have gone to the East, but the assassination of Philip of Swabia resulted in a temporary triumph of Innocent's policies in Germany when Otto of Brunswick was recognized as king. In November, 1209, however, the pope urged King Andrew of Hungary to go on a crusade if he believed that he could do so without danger to his throne,[74] and he continued to try to establish peace between John of England and Philip Augustus to facilitate the efforts they allegedly were making in behalf of the Holy Land.[75]

Late in December, 1212, the pope received a report of the death of Mary, Queen of Jerusalem and wife of John of Brienne, and on January 9, 1213, wrote a letter of condolence to the king. Grave injury would result to the Christian cause in the Holy Land if dissensions should arise among the princes as an aftermath of Mary's death, and

---

[73] *Ibid.*, CCXVI, cols. 36–37; M. L. de Mas Latrie (ed.), *Chronique d'Ernoul et de Bernard le Tresorier* (Société de l'histoire de France, Paris, 1871), XXXV, *passim*. See J. L. La Monte, *Feudal Monarchy in the Latin Kingdom of Jerusalem 1100 to 1291* (Cambridge, Mass., 1932), 46–47.

[74] Migne (ed.), *P.L.*, CCXIV, col. 1100.   [75] *Ibid.*, CCXVII, col. 213.

John accordingly was warned to refrain from attempts to enlarge his territories and urged to bear patiently such injuries as might be committed against him.[76] At the same time, Innocent pointed out to the Patriarch of Jerusalem that the death of the queen might produce "schisms and scandals." The prelate was directed to admonish all Christians to remain faithful to John and his infant daughter,[77] and the crusading orders also were ordered to defend the king against any challenge to his authority.[78]

There apparently was reason to fear that the King of Cyprus might take advantage of the situation to cause trouble. Innocent emphasized the lessons that Christians could learn from the fate that befell peoples divided against themselves in the face of aggression. The ruler of Cyprus was polluting the temple of the Lord by imprisoning King John's relatives and friends who had fled to Cyprus and "found suffering where they had hoped to find refuge from Saracen attacks." [79] Despite the pope's misgivings, however, there was no major attempt to question John's rights to rule the kingdom as regent for his daughter, Isabella, and later in the year he married Stephanie, daughter of King Leo of Armenia.[80]

Prospects for the crusading venture seemed brighter by the spring of 1213, when Grimaldus of Monte Sicilis and many allies took the cross. The pope applauded their devotion to the cause and bade them to be courageous despite the superior numbers of the enemy to be encountered. They were exhorted to "go as prudent men, and put their trust in the Lord—by Whose word the heavens were fashioned

[76] *Ibid.*, CCXVI, col. 738.　　　[77] *Ibid.*
[78] *Ibid.*, col. 737.　　　[79] *Ibid.*, cols. 736–37.
[80] La Monte, *Feudal Monarchy*, 55, 56, n. 1.

and for Whom the tempest ceases on land and sea when He commands." Archbishops in Lombardy and Tuscany were informed of Grimaldus' plans and ordered to endeavor to assure the success of his efforts. The prelates were directed to keep secret the preparations that were being made, "since a javelin seen in flight does less damage." [81]

Grimaldus, who apparently planned a small-scale attack as a prelude to the expected major invasion of the Holy Land, requested the pope to secure the aid of Venice for his enterprise. The pontiff accordingly wrote to the doge and counselors of that state, directing them to furnish ships, or at least to permit ships to be sold to the crusaders, since "it would be absurd if the power Venice had shown in temporal things should be wanting in the business of Christ." Publicity about the forthcoming attack on the Saracens was to be eschewed, as more effective results were anticipated if they could be taken by surprise. [82]

The response of the Venetian government was far from satisfactory. The doge agreed to furnish ships and other supplies as maritime cities were expected to do. But this favorable reaction to the pope's appeal was coupled with a request that the Venetian candidate for the vacant patriarchal chair at Constantinople be confirmed, and the pallium granted to the Archbishop-elect of Zara. Innocent, in August, 1213, praised the doge for his willingness to co-operate in the crusade but expressed astonishment that he should ask confirmation of the Venetian candidate for the patriarchate, when he knew that this matter had been under careful advisement ever since the irregular election that had followed the death of Thomas Morosini. In the Zara matter the pope declared that he was ready to bestow

[81] Migne (ed.), *P.L.*, CCXVI, col. 964.   [82] *Ibid.*, cols. 963-64.

the pallium whenever the doge swore to obey papal mandates in regard to Venetian excesses committed when that
city was captured and pillaged.[83]

About the same time, the pontiff wrote a long letter to
the Patriarch of Jerusalem, who was directed to allay dissensions in the Holy Land which might impede the crusade. King John, as well as all knights, pilgrims, and permanent residents of the Holy Land, should be summoned
to the task of liberating the land of Christ from the infidel
yoke. The pope was planning a general council, and since
he believed that the presence of the patriarch would be
helpful in furthering the crusading project, he was asked
to attend if his absence would not entail difficulties.[84]

Robert, Cardinal Priest of St. Stephen's, then was sent
as a legate to preach the crusade in France.[85] He was authorized to grant indulgences to all who came to hear the
word of the cross. The thorny problem of tournaments and
their effects on the crusades was left to his discretion, and
his expected arrival in France was announced to Philip
Augustus and his prelates.[86] The Abbot of Castelnau and
a deacon of Spires were appointed to represent the pope
in the matter of the crusade in the province of Mayence,[87]
and many similar commissions were issued, particularly in
Germany.[88]

General letters were sent to all Christian countries urging maximum efforts for the recovery of the Holy Land.
The pope declared that he was crying out as did Christ on
the cross. God easily could liberate the Holy Land from the
enemies of Christianity, but He imposed this task on the

[83] *Ibid.*, cols. 891–92.
[84] *Ibid.*, cols. 830–31.
[85] *Ibid.*, cols. 827–28.
[86] *Ibid.*, col. 827.
[87] *Ibid.*, col. 822.
[88] *Ibid.*, cols. 822–23; Potthast (ed.), *Regesta*, I, No. 4727.

faithful so that their devotion could be proved as gold is proved in the furnace. Plenary indulgence and facilitation of eternal salvation were promised those who went on the crusade at their own expense. Those who went at another's expense, or who paid the expenses of a crusader, were promised indulgences. Crusaders and their properties were placed under the protection of the pope. Oaths to make usurious payments were nullified, and usury already paid was ordered returned to those who had taken the cross. Whenever necessary, secular powers were directed to compel Jews to make such restitutions.

The pope himself promised to pay the expenses of clergy who went on the crusade and authorized them to continue to receive the incomes from their benefices for three years. Persons who took the vow to go on the crusade were to be accepted without examination of their fitness unless they were monks, since the pope dreamed of a great mass levy comparable with that for the First Crusade. Concessions that had been granted to Christians fighting the Moors in Spain and the Albigenses in France were revoked in order to swell the number of crusaders available for service in the East.

Stringent punishment was threatened against pirates who might interfere with the conduct of the crusading enterprise. Persons who dealt with them were ordered anathematized; indeed, failure to fight against them would be considered tantamount to aiding them. Christians who commanded ships in the service of Saracens or corsairs could be enslaved if they fell into the hands of loyal Christians, and this sentence was subsequently proclaimed in maritime cities every Sunday and feast day.

Constant efforts were prescribed to ensure divine aid

for the enterprise. Monthly processions with prayers at which offerings were to be taken for the financing of the crusade were ordered. With the elevation of the Host during the Mass, all were directed to prostrate themselves as the clergy chanted, "O God, the heathen are come into Thine inheritance." The service was to be concluded with the verse, "Let God arise, let His enemies be scattered; let them also that hate Him flee before Him." The celebrant then was to pray as follows: "God, Thou who disposeth everything by Thy admirable Providence, we pray beseechingly that Thou shouldst restore to the Christian cult the land which Thy eternal Son consecrated with His own blood and which is now held by the enemies of the cross, mercifully directing the vows of the faithful to its immediate liberation for the sake of eternal salvation." [89]

In 1214 legal privileges of pledged crusaders in France were specifically stated in response to complaints brought against the actions of the papal legate.[90] No crusader would be required to pay a tallage in city or country, even though he were a merchant, unless the tallage had been imposed prior to the time he took the cross, in which case his immunity would be effective a year later. Crusaders were likewise exempted for the duration of the crusade from suits for debts contracted subsequent to their assumption of the cross. Although persons who took the cross were not immune to criminal prosecutions involving danger to life or limb, they could not be arrested by the king's bailiffs for lesser offenses. Crusaders involved in suits against Christians who had not taken the cross were granted the right

---

[89] *Ibid.*, cols. 817–21. For concessions to crusaders in Provence, see Potthast (ed.), *Regesta*, I, Nos. 3510, 3511, 3512, 3640, 3783, 3820.

[90] Migne (ed.), *P.L.*, CCXVII, cols. 229–30.

to have their cases tried in ecclesiastical courts. Property of crusaders liable to tallage was not exempt, but crusaders who denied they possessed such property could appeal to their respective bishops. Taxes imposed on a commune for its defense had to be paid by the crusaders.[91] These provisions indicate that, although the crusaders still enjoyed substantial concessions, the rights of the king were fully safeguarded.[92]

Impetus was given to the development of crusading fervor in Germany by alleged miracles. A scholar of Cologne claimed that during the sixth feast before Pentecost, 1214, he said Mass in a meadow outside a town in Frisia. While the service was in progress, two white crosses were seen in the sky, it was said, and between them, illuminated by an eerie light, appeared the crucified Christ. Many ran forward to take the cross at the sight of this miraculous spectacle, which more than a hundred people declared they had seen. Some time later, on St. Boniface's day, a great white cross appeared where the saint had been martyred. This cross, allegedly seen by ten thousand people, moved through the sky as though "it showed the way to the sailing pilgrim to the promised land." The stories of these miracles seem to have been partly responsible for the muster of a large number of crusaders in Cologne, where it was reported, doubtless with exaggeration, that fifteen thousand were pledged, including nine thousand well-armed men, and thirty shiploads of supplies were gathered.[93]

Hostilities between England and France threatened to be a barrier to the success of the crusade. The pope, accordingly, in April, 1214, wrote to King John ordering that

[91] *Ibid.*, CCXVI, 239-40.   [92] Luchaire, *Innocent III*, IV, 285-86.
[93] Migne (ed.), *P.L.*, CCXVI, cols. 238-39.

firm peace be established between the two countries, since war "impeded succor for the Holy Land for which the king ardently aspired for the safety of the Christian people." Two mediators were chosen to treat with the kings for the arrangement of peace terms, and if they were unable to settle the matters at issue, the pope directed that his personal arbitration be accepted.[94] Nothing came of these efforts, and the battle of Bouvines provided the decision which arbitration failed to secure.

Formulation of plans for the crusade was one of the major objectives of the famous Fourth Lateran Council, which assembled in November, 1215. Crusaders who planned to go by ship were directed to depart in June, 1217, from Brindisi or Messina. Those preparing for an overland journey were instructed to leave at the same time. The pontiff promised to be present at the rendezvous of those taking passage at the designated ports to impart his blessing, while those going by land were directed to acquaint him more fully with their intentions so that legates could be sent to assist them.

All clergy were directed to teach crusaders to have the fear and love of God before their eyes. They were admonished to forswear jealousy and dissension so that "armed with spiritual and material weapons they might fight against the enemies of the faith, not vaunting their own power but trusting in divine strength." Clergy entrusted with the cure of souls were directed "studiously to preach the word of the cross to those whose care is committed to them, exhorting by Father, Son, and Holy Ghost, the one true eternal God, all kings and nobles that if they are not to participate personally in the crusade they will outfit a suit-

[94] *Ibid.*, col. 227.

able number of knights with expenses for three years, according to their means and in remission of their sins." Recusants were to be made to realize that they "would answer before a wrathful judge on an imminent day of strict judgment."

The pope announced that he offered £30,000 to defray the cost of the enterprise. Crusaders from the city of Rome, in addition to a ship furnished by the pontiff, were assigned 3,000 marks of silver to be distributed by the Patriarch of Jerusalem and the masters of the crusading orders upon their arrival in the Holy Land. All clergy were directed to pay one twentieth of their incomes for three years for the crusade, whereas the pope and the cardinals were pledged to a payment of a tenth for the same period. The usual concessions in regard to debts, immunity from tallage, and exemption from financial obligations incurred to Jews, were extended. Persons who traded with the Saracens were threatened with forfeiture of the entire amount earned by such transactions and the imposition of a fine from their private resources. No ships were permitted to sail to Saracen lands except those to be used for the crusade. Tournaments were forbidden for three years, and warfare among Christian princes and barons was banned on pain of excommunication and interdict. Forgiveness of sins was promised those who went on the crusade, furnished men, or "otherwise contributed according to their means and abilities to the furtherance of the work." [95] Wide latitude was given to preachers, including the power to absolve those guilty of arson or violence against the clergy, if such offenders

---

[95] C. J. Hefele and H. Leclerq (eds.), *Histoire des conciles*, 8 vols. (Paris, 1907), V, 2, 1930–95. See also Migne (ed.), *P.L.*, CCXVI, cols. 270–73; Potthast (ed.), *Regesta*, I, Nos. 5012, 5048, 5050; August Theiner (ed.), *Vetera monumenta Slavorum meridionalium historiam illustrantia*, I, 65–66.

wished to go on the crusade.[96] Relatives of those buried outside consecrated ground were permitted to transfer the remains of the deceased to suitable burial places if they took the cross.[97]

Preaching the crusade continued until Innocent's death on July 16, 1216. No great enthusiasm seems to have been aroused, and the ventures of Leopold of Austria and Andrew of Hungary were meager return for the great effort the pope had made to rally all Europe to the cause. In view of the indifference of the powerful secular rulers of the period, it is doubtful if more could have been achieved even with the pope's continued leadership. National rivalries, the growing rationalism of the schools, which was displacing blind devotion to a holy cause, and Innocent's own policy of intervention in temporal affairs all contributed to a spirit unfavorable to the universal undertaking which the pope, almost alone, so ardently desired.

[96] Potthast (ed.), *Regesta*, I, Nos. 4804, 4809.
[97] Edmond Martene (ed.), *Thesaurus Novus Anecdotorum*, 5 vols. (Paris, 1717), I, 850.

BIBLIOGRAPHICAL NOTE

SOURCES

The only large collection of Innocent III's letters is in
J. P. Migne (ed.), *Patrologiae cursus completus, Series Latina*, 221 vols. (Paris, 1844–1891), CCXIV–CCXVII. For
dates of the letters, however, it is necessary to rely largely
upon August Potthast (ed.), *Regesta Pontificum Romanorum*,
2 vols. (Berlin, 1875). For identification of prelates addressed
or referred to in the papal letters, Conrad Eubel, *Hierarchia
catholica medii aevi*, 3 vols. (Münster, 1898–1910), 2d ed. of
Vol. I (Münster, 1913), and P. B. Gams, *Series episcoporum
ecclesiae Catholicae* (Leipzig, 1931), are indispensable.

For letters of Innocent not included in the Migne, or for
better editions of some of the letters, the following were con-
sulted: Martin Bouquet (ed.), *Recueil des historiens des
Gaules et de la France*, 24 vols. (Paris, 1900–1904); Leopold
Delisle (ed.), "Lettres inédites d'Innocent III," *Bibliotheque
de l'école des chartes*, XXXIV (1873); E. G. Gersdorf and
C. F. von Posern-Klett (eds.), *Codex diplomaticus Saxoniae
regiae*, 3 vols. in 4 (Leipzig, 1864); Angelo Manrique (ed.),
*Cisterciensium seu verius ecclesiasticorum annalium a condito
Cistercio*, 4 vols. (Lyons, 1642–1659); F. A. Reiffenberg and
J. J. De Smet (eds.), *Monuments pour servir à l'histoire des
provinces de Namur, de Hainaut et de Luxembourg*, 2 vols.
(Brussels, 1844, 1869); August Theiner (ed.), *Vetera monumenta historica Hungariam sacram illustrantia*, 2 vols. (Rome,
1859); *id.*, *Vetera monumenta Slavorum meridionalium historiam illustrantia*, 2 vols. (Rome, 1863).

Letters in regard to monasteries are more scattered than for
any other topic in the present study. Many letters were pre-

served in monastic chartularies that were not registered, or for which only brief synopses were retained in the papal archives. For many of Innocent's letters dealing with the Cluniac Order one must consult the rare *Bullarium Sacri Ordinis Cluniacensis* (Lyons, 1680), edited by Pierre Symon, in the University of California Library, Berkeley. Other important source collections are: Georges Fejer (ed.), *Codex diplomaticus Hungariae ecclesiasticus ac civilis*, 11 vols. in 47 (Budapest, 1829–1844); C. L. Grotefend (ed.), *Urkunden-Buch des historischen Vereins für Niedersachsen*, 3 vols. (Hanover, 1846–1872); Colmar Grunhagen (ed.), *Regesten zur schlesischen Geschichte bis zum Jahre 1250, Codex diplomaticus Silesia*, 4 vols. in 7 (Breslau, 1868); Ernst Hauswirth (ed.), *Urkunden der Benedictiner-Abtei unserer Lieben Frau zu den Schotten in Wien, Fontes rerum Austriaricum, Diplomataria et acta*, 62 vols. (Vienna, 1849 ff.); Eduard von Kausler (ed.), *Urkunden-Buch Wirtembergisches*, 3 vols. (Stuttgart, 1849–1871); Jean LePaige (ed.), *Bibliotheca Praemonstratensis Ordinis*, 2 vols. (Paris, 1633); Gerold Meyer von Konau (ed.), *Die Regesten der ehemaligen Cistercienser-Abtei Cappel im Canton Zürich* (Chur, 1850); J. B. Mittarelli (ed.), *Annales Camaldulenses ordinis S. Benedicti*, 9 vols. (Venice, 1755–1773); P. H. Morice, *Mémoires pour servir de preuves à l'histoire ecclésiastique et civile de Bretagne*, 3 vols. (Paris, 1742); Karl Rossel (ed.), *Urkundenbuch der Abtei Eberbach im Rheingau*, 2 vols. (Wiesbaden, 1862–1870); J. N. Weis (ed.), *Urkunden des Cistercienser Stiftes Heiligenkreuz im Wiener Walde, Fontes rerum Austriaricum, Diplomataria et acta*; G. A. B. Wolff (ed.), *Chronik des Klosters Pforta*, 2 vols. (Leipzig, 1843).

Individual letters that are not contained in other collections as listed above may be found in: Guillaume Bessin, *Concilia Rotomagensis Provinciae*, 2 pts. (Rotomagi, 1717); Felice Bussi, *Istoria della citta di Viterbo* (Rome, 1742); J. H. Geslin de Bourgogne and Anatole de Barthelmy (eds.), *Anciens êveches de Bretagne*, 4 vols. (Paris and St. Brieuc, 1855–1864); J. G. Liljegren (ed.), *Svenskt Diplomatarium*, 5 vols.

in 8 (Stockholm, 1829–1867); Andrew von Meiller (ed.), *Regesta archiepiscoporum Salisburgensium* (Vienna, 1866); Saint-Rene Taillandier, *Histoire du chateau et du bourg de Blandy* (Paris, 1854); Benedetto Tromby (ed.), *Storia critic. cronol. diplomatica del patriarca s. Brunone e del suo ordine Cartusiana*, 10 vols. (Naples, 1733–1779); Ferdinand Ughelli, *Italia sacra ex edit. Nicolai Coleti*, 10 vols. (Venice, 1717–1722).

SECONDARY WORKS

General works on the papacy that have been useful in the preparation of this study are: J. N. Brischar, *Papst Innozenz III und seine Zeit* (Freiburg, 1893); George Krüger, *Das Papsttum: seine Idee und ihre Träger* (Tübingen, 1907); Felix Rocquain, *La papauté au moyen âge: Nicolas I., Gregoire VII., Innocent III., Boniface VIII.* (Paris, 1881).

Achille Luchaire, *Innocent III*, 6 vols. (2d ed.; Paris, 1911) retains its place as the leading general biography of Innocent III. Volume IV, *La question d'orient*, has been especially useful. Edouard Hürter, *Geschichte Papst Innocenz III und seine Zeitgenossen*, 4 vols. (Hamburg, 1834–1842), although obsolete on some topics, is still indispensable.

Works on ecclesiastical administration and its problems during the period have been of great usefulness. Among them the most important are: Hermann Baier, *Päpstliche Provisionen für niedere Pfründen bis zum Jahre 1304* (Münster, 1911); P. K. Baumgarten, *Aus Kanzlei und Kammer* (Freiburg, 1907); Ursmer Berlière, *Le recrutement dans les monasterès Benedictins au xiiie et xive siècles* (Brussels, 1924); Andrè Desprairies, *L'élection des évêques par les chapitres au xiiie siècle* (Paris, 1922); Ulrich Stutz, *Geschichte der Kirchlichen Benefizialwesens von seinen Anfänge bis auf die Zeit Alexander III* (Berlin, 1895). Heinrich Zimmermann, *Die päpstliche Legaten in der ersten Hälfte des 13 Jahrhunderts* (Paderborn, 1913), has been essential for the identification of the many legates that served Innocent III in important diplomatic capacities.

Reform activities of Innocent III are treated in summary form in Felix Rocquain, *La cour de Rome et l'esprit de reforme avant Luther* (Paris, 1893); and, of greater usefulness to this study, in Alberto Serafini, *I precedenti storici del concilio Lateranense IV (1215), Innocenzo III e la riforma religiosa agli inizii del sec. XIII* (Rome, 1917). Particular clerical abuses that necessitated reform efforts are treated in: Albert Houtin, *Courte histoire du célibat ecclésiastique* (Paris, 1929); H. C. Lea, *An Historical Sketch of Sacerdotal Celibacy* (2d ed.; Boston, 1884); Selmar Scheler, *Sitten und Bildung der französischen Geistlichkeit nach den Briefen Stephans von Tournai* (Berlin, 1915); R. A. Ryder, *Simony, A Historical Synopsis and Commentary* (Washington, D.C., 1931); W. A. Weber, *A History of Simony in the Christian Church* (Baltimore, 1909). In view of the close connection between virtually all of Innocent III's policies and the German Civil War, Richard Schwemer, *Innocenz III und die deutsche Kirche während des Thronstreites von 1198–1208* (Strassburg, 1882), is helpful.

Important background material for the chapter on Eastern Europe was secured from: Clemens Brandenburger, *Pölnische Geschichte* (Leipzig, 1907); C. A. Ferrario, *Storia dei Bulgari* (Milan, 1940); Balint Homan, *Geschichte des Ungarischen Mittelalters*, 2 vols. (Berlin, 1943); Constantin Jirecêk, *Geschichte der Serben*, 2 vols. (Gotha, 1911); Edouard Krakowski, *Histoire de la Pologne* (Paris, 1934); Edouard Sayous, *Histoire generale des Hongrois*, 2 vols. (Paris, 1900).

Important works on the Fourth Crusade are Louis Brehier, *L'église et l'orient au moyen âge* (3d ed.; Paris, 1911); Ernst Gerland, *Geschichte der lateinischen Kaiserreiches von Konstantinopel: Geschichte der Kaiser Baldwin I und Heinrich I 1204–1216* (Hamburg, 1905); J. L. La Monte, *Feudal Monarchy in the Latin Kingdom of Jerusalem 1100 to 1291* (Cambridge, Mass., 1932); William Miller, *Essays on the Latin Orient* (Cambridge, 1921); Walter Norden, *Das Papsttum und Byzanz* (Berlin, 1903).

INDEX

050884

ST. MARY'S COLLEGE OF MARYLAND
ST. MARY'S CITY, MARYLAND